The Assemblies Res[ource]

Canterbury Diocesan
RE Resource Centre

SPCK

Published in Great Britain in 2001
Society for Promoting Christian Knowledge
Holy Trinity Church
Marylebone Road
London NW1 4DU

Copyright © SPCK 2001

'The cook's tale' (page 47) and 'Victorians – Learning from the past' (page 86) are copyright © Kate Fleming 2001

All rights reserved. No part of this book may be reproduced or transmitted in any form or by any means, electronic or mechanical, including photocopying, recording, or by any information storage and retrieval system, without permission in writing from the publisher.

Bible quotations unless otherwise stated
are from the Good News Bible published by
The Bible Societies/HarperCollins Publishers UK Ltd
© American Bible Society 1966, 1971, 1976, 1992.

British Library Cataloguing-in-Publication Data

A catalogue record for this book
is available from the British Library

ISBN 0-281-05418-5

Typeset by Wilmaset Ltd, Birkenhead, Wirral
Printed in Great Britain by
The Cromwell Press, Trowbridge, Wilts

Contents

Foreword   v

AUTUMN TERM   1
New school year   3
The seasons and God's promise   6
The Good Samaritan   8
Bravery   10
Psalm 19 – A song about the whole creation   13
Football   17
George Frideric Handel – Don't give up!   19
Water   22
Shadrach, Meshach and Abednego   24
Gift tags – Everyone has something to offer   28
Families   31
Prayer   34
All together now! – The expressive arts   37
Winter   39
No room . . .   43
The cook's tale   47

SPRING TERM   51
Epiphany   53
Wolfgang Amadeus Mozart – Never a dull moment!   57
Why worry? (1)   60
Why worry? (2)   62
The Bible   66
Mums   69
The lost son   71
Spirituals – A brighter day   77
The wonder of creation   80
Victorians – Celebrating the past   83
Victorians – Learning from the past   86
Wise or foolish – Making choices   90
Stronger together   93
Easter 1 – Turning the tables   95
Easter 2 – Carrying the cross   98
Easter 3 – Sunday morning   101

SUMMER TERM 103
Psalm 150 – A song of praise   105
Tummy ache   108
Light and darkness   111
Antonio Vivaldi   113
Feeling safe   116
Making things   119
Pilgrimages   121
Alone – Sometimes I want to be on my own   124
Samuel in the Temple – Listening to God   127
Breath and breathing   130
Perseverance   133
Looking after God's world – Or 'name that job!'   135
Pulling together   138
Try your best – Don't worry!   141
Words and how we use them   144
School sports   147

Indexes   151
   Authors   151
   Biblical references   151
   Themes and content   151

Foreword

Welcome to the book of the web site! Since its launch in September 1999, the SPCK Assemblies web site has become something of a phenomenon, receiving over 50,000 page impressions a month and used by busy teachers and ministers across the UK – and some further afield. Feedback from users tells us that what they like about the site is the easy and swift access to resources, the contribution of inventive writers, the 'mix and match' adaptability of the assemblies and the regular updates of new material. What they like most of all, however, is the fact that all the ideas are tried and tested – sometimes to destruction which can seem dangerously close at times in the hectic school environment!

These assemblies are all written by people who are used to standing in front of children and attempting to deliver that unique mix of social cohesion, notices for the day, ethical message, thinking time and religious 'glue' suitable for a wide and diverse range of backgrounds; and all in a few precious moments. Assembly is difficult and our writers and readers know that. If not every idea hits the spot for you, most will offer some idea and inspiration and every one will be useful to someone, somewhere. The success of www.assemblies.org.uk, both in terms of numbers of users and of positive feedback, suggests that the site is doing enough right, enough of the time, to make a significant contribution to the school life of the country.

With such a success in the new technology world, why are we now publishing a book of selected material from the site? The foremost reason is that you asked for it! We've had many requests from users of the assembly site to provide some of the assemblies in more permanent form. We recognize that the ever-changing web site, although it does include some permanently available assemblies, offers a different kind of resource. Even if enterprising teachers do print off their favourite assemblies and file them for future use, there's something about a well printed and bound book that provides a more appropriate way of storing resources that you intend to use again and again in the future.

So we've taken the best of the assemblies from the first year and a half of the site and edited them for book publishing. The selection has been difficult, for while the web site has a large number of monthly updates (two new assemblies per week during term-time), and the ability to provide rapid response material at times of tragedy or national significance, the book version must offer more widely applicable material. Yet we didn't want to coalesce around a centre ground of common themes and approaches and miss out on some of the more inventive or surprising ideas. You'll find Bible-based stories and themes alongside ethical issues. There's participatory material as well as drama and poetry. We've tried to marry good writing with assemblies that are practical and can be adapted to your own style.

Making the most of the ideas

Exciting, lively and relevant content are vital elements of a good assembly, but they are brought to life by the presentation. When preparing assemblies, think about the following.

Use of space

Consider the space in which you and others will present the assembly, and also where the children will sit. Tailor the space to suit the theme and style of the assembly. Does the assembly include drama, dance or a music performance? If so, can everyone see and hear? Will it be easy for the performers to find their space, props and instruments? Are they too distant or too close to the rest of the children – either can be intimidating and off-putting to those unused to performance.

Think about trying some different styles – perhaps an assembly in the round or an arena (children on three sides) approach. Perhaps the 'performers' can be dotted around the space so that different voices and sounds emanate from various parts of the hall. Why not create a pathway of PE mats that you can walk during the assembly, taking you through the space in which the children are sitting – it all adds variety and can be appropriate to the theme.

Visual focus

What will the children look at during the assembly? Often the plan includes visual elements such as drama, or a music performance or active story-telling. At other times it is appropriate to think about some form of visual focus:

- A flip-chart picture (simple happy/sad faces are used in a number of assemblies to indicate feelings in stories).
- Overhead projector image(s).
- A group of objects appropriate to the theme.

If you do create a visual focus, think about:

- Is it large enough to be seen from the back of the space?
- Do those at the extreme edges have a clear view?
- Is it complementary to the rest of the assembly, or distracting?
- Can you use intriguing objects that will only make sense as you refer to them during the assembly?

Use of voice

Teachers and ministers probably know more about this than any other professions. You will probably be used to filling a space with sound when necessary, then dropping your voice to make the listeners attentive. Assemblies use all your natural classroom (or church) management skills, but they also provide opportunities to try some different ways of doing things.

You could try a dialogue with two contrasting voices – perhaps a male and a female teacher at different sides of the space. If you or another assembly leader can develop a range of voices for story-telling, this can also add variety and increase interest.

The use of children's voices can be more problematic. The easy option is to go for those with loud voices who enjoy performance, and certainly such children should be given opportunities to use their gifts. Essentially, however, assembly is about something other than performance; its focus lies in shared time and shared experience. Those children who are less at home with speaking or doing in front of a large group should be supported to do so. See the 'Use of space' suggestions above for ideas about bringing them closer to the rest of the children, reducing the need for a 'big voice'.

You could also consider using a microphone if appropriate or (in the case of prayers, meditations, or other prepared presentation), pre-recording individuals' contributions and playing them on cassette at the appropriate moments.

One thing you can be sure of: all the ideas in this book are tried and tested, by the authors and by the thousands of users of the web site and the children who've been on the 'receiving end'. The assemblies within simply await your unique contribution to bring them to life.

GORDON LAMONT
Editor, www.assemblies.org.uk

Autumn Term

NEW SCHOOL YEAR
By Gill Hartley

Suitable for Whole School

Aim

To reflect on the new opportunities and challenges a new school year will bring.

Preparation and materials

- Prepare the story of Zacchaeus. Use our version below, or another in language appropriate to the youngest children present, e.g. the Good News Bible or *The Beginner's Bible* (Kingsway Publications).
- A CD or cassette of quiet background music suitable for reflection.

Assembly

1. Ask the children what is new today. For example, some new people (new children and possibly new members of staff), some people wearing new clothes, a new school year, a new term. If this is not the first assembly of the school year, look for other things new, such as a new day, a new week, etc.
2. Read the story of Zacchaeus (based on Luke 19) – someone who changed for the better after meeting Jesus.

    The Story of Zacchaeus
    by Gordon Lamont

    Jesus was busy teaching and healing and he came to a place called Jericho. A huge crowd came out to see him and in the crowd was a man named Zacchaeus. He wasn't very popular in Jericho because he was a tax collector who took the people's money and gave it to the Romans. Now Zacchaeus desperately wanted to see Jesus, to find out what all the fuss was about. But he had a problem – he was too short to see over the heads of the people in the crowd. It looked like he was going to miss out.

Then he saw the answer – a tree, right by the spot where Jesus would pass. Quick as a flash, Zacchaeus climbed the tree. Just as he did, Jesus saw him and said, 'Come on down, Zacchaeus. I need to stay in your house tonight.'

Lucky Zacchaeus was so pleased and excited that he almost fell out of the tree in surprise.

A lot of people in the crowd were not so pleased. They started shouting that Jesus shouldn't be seen with a person like Zacchaeus, a tax collector!

Zacchaeus heard them and dusted himself off and went straight up to Jesus.

'I have an announcement to make,' he said. 'I will give half of everything I own to the poor. *And*, everyone that I have ever cheated can have their money back – four times over.'

Zacchaeus had a new friend, Jesus – and a new way of life.

3. Sum up the story by reminding the children that each day is a new chance – a chance to be different and a chance to make new friends. If we have done things we're sorry about we can begin afresh each new day. This is even more true of a new school year!

Time for reflection

Play some quiet music as background for this guided reflection.

> Think about what this new year might be like for you.
> Are you looking forward to it?
> Are you frightened of anything?
> Are there things you're nervous about?
> Are there things you'd like to do better than last year?
> What new chance would you like this year? How would you like to be different?
>
> Dear God,
> Help us when we are frightened because we have to go somewhere new.

Help us not to panic when we have to do something new.
Help us not to be frightened of making a mistake.
Help us to remember other people's feelings, especially if they are new to our school.
Help us always to do our best.
Amen.

Song

'Thank you, Lord, for this new day' (*Come and Praise*, 32)

THE SEASONS AND GOD'S PROMISE
By Jill Fuller

Suitable for Whole School

Aim

To help the children recognize the rhythm of the changes of the seasons. To draw their attention to the Christian belief of God's promise of seedtime and harvest.

Preparation and materials

- Try to have the following available: fallen leaves from trees, a torch, an item of warm clothing, like a scarf or gloves. (The visual aids are not essential, particularly if seasonal weather can be seen or heard during the assembly!)
- Prepare the Bible reading below.

Assembly

1. Using your visual aids as a prompt, ask the children what they notice about the time of the year: leaves falling from the trees, flowers dying back; people making bonfires and clearing gardens; shorter days, fewer hours of sunlight, so we are turning lights on earlier and will need to use torches; less sunshine and warmth, so we will need to look out our gloves and scarves.
2. Ask the children to name the season we are moving from, through and into (summer, autumn and winter). Which season do they think will follow winter?
3. Mention other natural rhythms of our lives, for example day and night, the ebb and flow of tides, the phases of the moon, planting seeds and harvesting crops, life cycles (being born, growing up and dying).
4. Remind the children of the story of Noah and the flood, and

how after the flood God made a promise that seedtime and harvest would always occur. The rainbow in the sky would be a sign of this promise.
5. Read Genesis 8.22 and 9.12–15. The following version is adapted from the Good News Bible.

> As long as the world exists, there will be a time for planting and a time for harvest. There will always be cold and heat, summer and winter, day and night . . . As a sign of this everlasting [promise] which I am making with you . . . I am putting my [rain] bow in the clouds. It will be the sign of my [promise] with the world. Whenever I cover the sky with clouds and the rainbow appears, I will remember my promise to you.

Time for reflection

You may choose to remind children that Christians believe in a loving Creator who gave us a beautiful world to enjoy and who keeps his promises to us season by season.

Song

'God has promised' (*Come and Praise*, 31)

Curriculum links

- English: Make an anthology of poems about the seasons. Weather sayings.
- Science: Life cycles.
- IT: Creating a rainbow.
- RE: The story of Noah and God's promise.
- History: How weather has been recorded.
- Geography: The effects of seasons and weather on people, recognizing seasonal patterns in the weather.
- Art/DT: Different artists' interpretations of the seasons.
- Music: Listen to Vivaldi's *Four Seasons*.
- SMSC: Discussion about moral responsibility for the planet and how human behaviour affects weather patterns.

THE GOOD SAMARITAN
By Barbara Kazer

Suitable for Whole School

Aim

To encourage children to think about helping others, whether they like them or not.

Preparation and materials

- Prepare the story of the Good Samaritan (Luke 10.25–37) to tell it in your own words.
- Ask four children to take part, a few minutes before the assembly. They will perform a simple mime while you talk for them. Alternatively you can act out the characters yourself. You will also need a chair for the mime.
- Introductory music: 'Air' from J. S. Bach's Orchestral Suite No. 3 (*Air on a G string*).

Assembly

1. Play Bach's 'Air' as the children assemble.
2. Greet the children and explain that you are going to talk about helping others. Ask about the people they help. Discuss how it is easy to help people that they like. Suggest that they think, to themselves, about how they feel about helping people they don't like. For instance, if the class bully falls and cuts their leg, and there is no one else around. Or perhaps a friend they've just quarrelled with walks off and drops their favourite pencil.
3. Many of us would think, 'serve them right'. Ask the children to be honest and think to themselves of a time when they have thought that.
4. Suggest to the children that their first thought should be to

help. Say that Jesus told a story about helping. He called it being a Good Samaritan. Explain that in those days the Samaritans and the Jews hated each other. (You could draw comparison with current news events showing the hatred between people of different races and religions today.)

5. Tell the story of the Good Samaritan while the four children mime the actions.

   Child 1, a Jew (like Jesus), staggers on and flops on to the chair. Explain that Child 1 has been mugged and left in a deserted place.
   Child 2 walks by, and sees but ignores the victim. Explain that Child 2 is a priest and of the same faith as the mugged person.
   Child 3 does the same. Explain that Child 3 is a Levite, another religious person of the same faith.
   Child 4 walks on, stops, helps the victim up and takes them to the side of hall. Explain that Child 4 is a Samaritan, who looks after the victim, even paying their medical bills, until they are well again.

6. Ask the children to say who was the helper in the story. Remind them that the Samaritan helped the enemy he hated. Jesus was showing that we should help everyone, not just those people we like.

7. Ask the children to think to themselves of someone they don't much like and suggest they try to help them next time.

Time for reflection

Dear God,
Let us think of those who need our help.
Let us try, at school and at home, to be a Good Samaritan
by helping everyone, even those people we don't much like.
Amen.

Song

'Cross over the road, my friend' (*Come and Praise*, 70)

BRAVERY
By Gill Hartley

Suitable for Whole School

Aim

To reflect on the need for bravery in everyday life.

Preparation and materials

- A picture of a knight in armour.
- A CD or cassette of quiet music for use as a background to reflection.

Assembly

1. Show the picture of a knight in armour, and talk about it, explaining in simple terms the various pieces of armour and weapons, etc. (If no picture is available, ask the children if they can describe a knight, bringing out the same points in the discussion.)
   Remind the children that the armour and weapons were used for fighting battles, and ask them if they expect to need any of them today. Do they expect to be involved in the sort of battles that would make such things necessary? (Hopefully you will be able to establish that they do not!)
2. Sing the song, 'When a knight won his spurs'. Or, if the song is not known to the children, read it to them as a poem.
3. Talk about the song with the children. Ask them if the songwriter expected to be fighting battles. (Both answers are possible to this question, i.e. 'No' because there are no more giants or dragons; and 'Yes' because there are still things to fight against.)
   Ask the children what sort of things the songwriter expected to have to fight against. (You are looking for answers such as

anger, greed, etc.) Ask where he expected to have to do the fighting – on a battlefield, or inside his head? Confirm that the song is about fighting inner battles, and that everyone has to fight from time to time against the temptation to do wrong things.
4. Ask if any of the children would like to share their experiences of times when they have had to be brave in fighting an inner battle against the temptation to do something they knew they should not do. Sum up the incidents shared by pointing out that the battles the children have just referred to do not need metal armour like the knight wore, but a different sort of armour altogether.
5. Read some verses from the letter Paul wrote to the new Christians in Ephesus, either from Ephesians 6.11, 14–17, in a modern translation of the New Testament, or use the paraphrase below:

> Put on all of God's armour:
> Instead of a belt, surround yourself with truth.
> Use honesty to protect you, instead of chain mail.
> Use faith as a shield.
> Take God's promise to care for you as a helmet, and God's words as your sword.
> With all of this you will be able to be strong inside.

Time for reflection

Play some quiet music as a background for this guided reflection.

> Think about being brave . . .
> We have to be brave to do all kinds of things every day . . .

(Here mention some of the situations the children may have shared in the assembly, or substitute some of your own, such as: telling the truth, saying sorry, trying something new, doing something we don't want to, not doing something we want to.)

> Dear God,
> Help us to be brave and do what is right,
> to stand up for what is good,
> and to speak the truth.
> **Amen.**

🎵 Song

'When a knight won his spurs' (*Come and Praise*, 50)

PSALM 19 – A SONG ABOUT THE WHOLE CREATION

By Jill Fuller

Suitable for Whole School

Aim

To introduce the concept of the psalms. To explore Psalm 19 (verses 1–6) with its theme of creation.

Note: This assembly shares the same general introduction to the psalms as that on Psalm 150 (see page 105).

Preparation and materials

- You will need a Bible large enough to be seen easily by everyone.
- Practise reading Psalm 19.1–6, or rehearse a child to read it. The Good News Bible version is included below. You can of course use another translation.

Assembly

1. Hold up the Bible and ask the children if they know what it is called. Explain that the one book, the Bible, is really a collection of many smaller books. Explain that there are two main sections and ask children if they know what these are called (Old Testament and New Testament).
2. Explain how the Old Testament tells mainly the story of the Jewish people before Jesus, and the New Testament tells the story of the life of Jesus and also contains letters and describes events in the early Christian Church.
3. Say that today we are looking at a book in the Old Testament called The Book of Psalms. The Hebrew title of the book, *sepher tehilim*, means 'book of praises'; the English word

'psalm' comes from the Greek word *psalmoi* meaning 'songs accompanied by string music'.

4. Use some of the following information to explain about the psalms:

   The Book of Psalms is rather like a hymnbook. Just as a hymnbook contains songs and hymns written at different dates, so the psalms were written at different times in Old Testament history.

   There are 150 psalms. We do not know for sure who wrote them. People think there were many authors, but generally David, the shepherd boy who fought Goliath and later became king, is thought to have written about half of them.

   It is likely that the psalms were usually sung and sometimes accompanied with music. In the Hebrew text, a word meaning musical interlude, *selah*, often occurs (e.g. Psalm 46).

   The psalms were used in worship both at the Temple in Jerusalem and in synagogues (explain Jewish places of worship if necessary). Jesus would have known the Book of Psalms.

   The early Church probably used psalms in public services. They are still used today by both Jewish and Christian people in synagogues and churches.

   The psalms are almost like talks with God, and contain many moods. Sometimes the writer is joyful and full of praise and trust, at others desperately sad and questioning God.

5. Introduce Psalm 19.1–6 as being a wonderful description of how the writer saw the glory of God in the sky. Ask the children to listen to the writer's description of the movement of the sun in the sky, the sunrise and sunset. If appropriate, ask them to close their eyes. Read Psalm 19.1–6 and reflect together on what everyone present, children and staff, enjoys about the description.

   > How clearly the sky reveals God's glory!
   > How plainly it shows what he has done!
   > Each day announces it to the following day;
   > each night repeats it to the next.
   > No speech or words are used, no sound is heard;
   > yet their message goes out to all the world

and is heard to the ends of the earth.
God made a home in the sky for the sun;
it comes out in the morning like a happy bridegroom,
like an athlete eager to run a race.
It starts at one end of the sky and goes across to the other.
Nothing can hide from its heat.

6. Encourage the children to share experiences of when the sight of a sunrise, sunset, or starry night has led them to feel wonder and amazement – for instance, staying up especially late, being out on bonfire night, seeing the sun reflected in the sea, etc.
7. Explain that Christians believe that a loving God created the world with all its wonders for us to both share and care for.
8. Sing verse 1 of 'Praise the Lord, you heavens' (*Come and Praise*, 35).

Time for reflection

As the person who wrote this psalm recognized the wonder of God in the created world around,
so may we today be able to see the beauty and wonder of creation.
Amen.

Song

'Praise the Lord, you heavens' (*Come and Praise*, 35)

Curriculum links

- English: Write a description of a sky the children have enjoyed: sunrise or sunset, night-time or a day when the clouds were particularly impressive.
- Science: Find out about how a compass works and how sailors used the movements of the sun, moon and stars to navigate.
- RE: Discover about the worship of sun gods in some religious traditions.
- Art/DT: Make a collection of pictures of different ways artists have depicted sunrise or sunset or skies.

- Music: Listen to music that evokes the sun, moon, or planets, e.g. Holst's *The Planets Suite*, or Debussy's *Clair de Lune*.

FOOTBALL
By Gill Hartley

Suitable for KS2

Aim

To reflect on and to reaffirm important values.

Preparation and materials

- Pens and a large sheet of paper and Blu-tack, or a flip-chart. Write in large letters:
  G
  O
  A
  L

Assembly

1. Ask the children which football teams they support. Who are their favourite players? If possible, discuss with them briefly a current important football event. Ask what a football team has to do to win a match. Hopefully someone will mention scoring goals!
2. Discuss the meaning of the word 'goal' as something to be aimed for. We sometimes talk about having a goal in life – something we want to do, somewhere we want to end up, an ambition.
3. Ask the children what their goals in life are. What do they want to be when they grow up? Share some of their ideas. Ask them if adults can have a goal in life – after all, they're already grown up!
4. Explain that you have a goal to suggest for all grown ups. Put up the large sheet of paper, or reveal the flip-chart sheet, on which you have written:

G
O
A
L

While the children are watching, write in:

G rowing
O lder
A nd
L ovelier

(This will probably produce some laughter!)

5. Ask the children if they think that everyone can be beautiful. Hopefully they will agree that they cannot! Point out that this does not prevent everyone from being a 'lovely person'. Ask them what they think that means. Do they know anyone they would describe as a 'lovely person'? What is that person like?
6. Pick out some of the qualities the children describe and remind them that they are values which are important in their school, and also things which people from many religions believe are important to God. Many of these values also help in a team game like football!

Time for reflection

Dear God,
Thank you for the fun we have watching and playing football.
Help us always to play fair.
Give us the skill we need to aim straight for the goal,
not just in our matches, but in life as well.
Help us to discover what we should aim for in life
so that we may grow into the sort of person others are glad to know.
Amen.

Song

'Give me oil in my lamp' (*Come and Praise*, 43)

GEORGE FRIDERIC HANDEL – DON'T GIVE UP!

By Margaret Liversidge

Suitable for Whole School

Aim

To enable children to recognize that the 'gifts' and interests they have are special and that, with perseverance, these can prove of lasting value in life.

Preparation and materials

- A board or card showing the words 'George Frideric Handel 1685–1759'.
- If possible, pictures of the instruments mentioned: organ, harpsichord, violin, oboe.
- Introductory music by Handel to play as the children are gathering, e.g. *Music for the Royal Fireworks* or *Water Music*.

Assembly

1. Ask the children to think of and tell you about things that they recognize they are good at: sport, drawing, playing the recorder, dancing, etc. Discuss briefly what they are doing, or could do, to improve and build on this talent.
2. Ask if there's ever been a time when they have really wanted to do something related to their interest but it hasn't been possible. You might need to give some examples, such as conflict with homework or with the needs/wishes of friends or other family members.

    Explain that you are going to tell the children about a boy who felt just like this when his father disapproved of his interest in music. Point out at this stage that although it was

difficult for the boy, he persevered and as a result became a very famous musician.
3. From the board or chart practise saying together George Frideric Handel's name. If you used introductory music, explain that Handel composed the music they heard before the assembly.
4. Tell the story of Handel as follows:

> Once there was a boy who absolutely loved music. In fact, he was so talented that as he grew older he learnt to play the organ, the harpsichord, the violin, and the oboe, and he composed a huge amount of music as well. His name was (*children join in with* . . .) George Frideric Handel.
>
> George's mother recognized that he seemed to have a very special musical talent. She was a good lady who believed in God. She went to church to worship God with other people. From a very early age young George was influenced by his mother's Christian faith. He went to church with her, and learned to appreciate the use of beautiful music for worshipping God. He learned to play the organ.
>
> But George's father wanted his son to work in the courts as a lawyer when he grew up. He thought George's interest in music was just a child's game, a waste of time and effort. At least George knew that his mother was on his side!
>
> One day George's father was surprised to receive a summons from a very important duke. George's father couldn't possibly imagine why he had been commanded to go and speak to the duke. As it happened, the duke had been at a church service where he had been thrilled by the organ playing of, guess who, young George! And George's father hadn't even known that his son had been playing the organ.
>
> The duke told George's father that the boy was obviously musically talented and that such talent should be encouraged. So from that day onwards, George was supported in his music by both his parents and he became a famous musician and composer of music.

5. Explain to the children that because he stuck at it, even when his own father discouraged him, Handel's music became his lifetime's work, and 250 years later we consider the music he wrote to be some of the most lively and enjoyable there is.

Time for reflection

Ask the children to reflect on their special gifts/talents or the things they specially like to do. Encourage them to consider that it is worth persevering to get better at what they wish to do.

> Dear God,
> Thank you for our special gifts and interests.
> Thank you for parents and teachers who help us along the way.
> Please enable us to keep going when the going gets tough.
> **Amen.**

Song

'Simple gifts' (*Come and Praise 2*, 97)

Curriculum links

Music, PSHE, Geography

WATER
By Patrice Baldwin

Suitable for Whole School

Aim

To guide children towards an understanding of water as a symbol of life. To reflect upon the fact that water is not readily available to all people in the world.

Preparation and materials

- A cardboard box with a glass of water hidden inside, which should be placed centrally so that everyone can see it.
- Introductory music: Handel's *Water Music*.

Assembly

1. Play part of Handel's *Water Music* as the children assemble.
2. Tell the children that inside the cardboard box is the most precious thing in the whole world. Ask them to suggest what it might be. Do not tell them whether they are right or wrong.
3. Take out the glass of water and invite a child to come up and drink half of it in front of everybody.
4. Tell the children that in some parts of the world a drink of water can be a dangerous thing. Water can spread disease and make people ill. Ask them how the child who just drank the water knew it would be safe to drink. We know that our water is treated to cleanse it.
5. Tell everyone that the water the child drank has already been used before many times. Water falls as rain. Some is collected and used by people. Some evaporates and falls again as rain. Ask them to think about and give examples of how they have used water so far today, e.g. washing, flushing the toilet, cooking, etc.

6. Tell them that in many parts of the world people use rainwater and river water (or maybe water from a well) and have no way of cleaning it. In other parts of the world there is no water at all. Sometimes people are drinking water that they know is unsafe and dangerous to their health, but they have no choice.
7. Invite the child to drink the rest of the glass of water.

Time for reflection

Ask the children to close their eyes. Guide their reflection with the following words:

> Without water there would be no plants.
> Without water there would be no animals.
> Without water there would be no people.
> Without water there would be no life.
> Let us be thankful for the water of life.

Follow this with a few moments of silence.

Songs

'Water of life' (*Come and Praise*, 2)
'Think of a world without any flowers' (*Come and Praise*, 17)

Curriculum links
- Science: Life and living processes.
- Geography: Weather and climate and the water cycle.

SHADRACH, MESHACH AND ABEDNEGO
By Ronni Lamont

Suitable for KS2

Aim

To consider standing up for what we believe to be right and true.

Preparation and materials

- The story is found in Daniel 3. This is an instant drama assembly, and you are the narrator.
- The king and the statue can be played by adults, all the other parts by children. Pick out the children to play these parts when you get there in the story.
- You also need someone who can play some fanfare-type music – the same few bars, several times.
- Decide how you will pronounce those names, and stick to it!
- You need a golden crown that an adult will wear as the king.
- If you can make/borrow/steal a large statue all the better! If not, get an adult to pose.

Assembly

1. Explain that the story is set in Babylon. About 2,500 years ago, it was the greatest city in the world. If you go to the British Museum in London, you can see all sorts of things – doors, statues – from the city that date from the time that we are talking about.

    At that time, there were lots of people living in Babylon who were exiles – captured through wars and taken to the city. Among those people were:

Shadrach (*ask for a volunteer*)
Meshach (*another volunteer*)
and Abednego (*another volunteer*).

Shadrach, Meshach and Abednego were Jewish, and worshipped their own God, who they believed was the one true God. This is the God that Jewish people still worship, and so do Muslims and Christians.

2. Recruit some soldiers to stand by the king. Enter the king, who sits down. Explain that the king had a strange name – Nebuchadnezzar. He had a huge, tall statue made, and set it on the ground outside the city. He told everyone that when the band played, everyone had to worship the statue.

Musician(s) play short fanfare or similar.

Explain that everyone bowed down to the statue.

Soldiers enact this, but Shadrach, Meshach and Abednego don't.

3. Continue the story:

The king was very cross with Shadrach, Meshach and Abednego, and told them to worship his statue, but they wouldn't.

Musician(s) play short fanfare – soldiers bow again.

'We worship the true God, the God of Israel,' said Shadrach, Meshach and Abednego. When the king threatened to kill them for not worshipping his statue, they said, 'Fair enough. Perhaps our God will save us, perhaps he won't. But we believe it is wrong to worship your statue. We're sticking with our God, the God of Israel.'

King Nebuchadnezzar grew very angry. He ordered his soldiers to go and stoke up his furnace.

Soldiers mime stoking furnace, wiping brows, etc.

Then the king ordered the soldiers to tie up Shadrach, Meshach and Abednego and to throw them into the fire!

Soldiers tie them up and push them into the fire.

It was so hot, that the soldiers died from the heat!

> *Soldiers keel over.*

> After a while, the king went to have a look and see how our heroes were doing.

> *The king wanders towards 'furnace' area, where Shadrach, Meshach and Abednego have been joined by another person.*

> They were fine, absolutely fine. The king couldn't understand what was going on. He'd put three men into the fire, and now there were four, and none of them were burnt at all!

4. Ask the children who they think the fourth person is, and where he or she has come from.
5. Continue the story:

   > The king ordered the three men out of the furnace, and asked them how they had survived. They told him that God had sent an angel to care for them. King Nebuchadnezzar was so impressed that he declared himself a follower of the same God, the God of Shadrach, Meshach and Abednego.

   > *Musician(s) play short fanfare or similar. This time no one bows to the statue.*

6. Talk about the story, pointing out that God saved Shadrach, Meshach and Abednego, even though they said that he might not. Ask the children if they know of any people who died because they wouldn't do what another person was trying to force them to do. Do they know of anyone who wouldn't say that they believed something when they didn't? Perhaps they know of people who died because they believed in a way of life, or a faith, that wasn't the same as everyone else? Ideally prompt people like Jesus, Martin Luther King, Gandhi.
7. Explain that we call these people 'martyrs': people who are prepared to die for something that they hold very dear. We probably won't have to do that, but point out that we all have our beliefs. As we grow up, we need to hold on to the things that we know are good and true, and stand up for them even when others are saying they aren't true.

Time for reflection

Loving God,
Help us to stand up for what we know to be true, and good, and right,
even when it's hard to do that.
Help us to know that you are with us, even though we can't see you.
Amen.

Song

'There are hundreds of sparrows' (*Come and Praise*, 15; *Hymns Old and New*, 498)

GIFT TAGS – EVERYONE HAS SOMETHING TO OFFER

By Jill Fuller

Suitable for Whole School

Aim

To help children recognize what they have to offer to each other and to the community.

Preparation and materials

Choose a number of children from different years (and perhaps a staff member) to participate (the nominees). Then ask other people (children and staff) who know the nominees to prepare a few sentences to describe each person's particular gift. Make sure there is a range of offerings, which could include school subjects such as music, mathematics, sport, and gifts of character such as courage, friendliness, kindness, patience. For example:

> This is Sheena. She is particularly good at team games. She always encourages us and helps us to do well.
> This is Paul. He is especially good at listening. He is the kind of person everyone can talk to and share their worries with.
> This is David. He is great at painting and this is something he painted recently.
> This is Mary. She is fantastically quick at mental arithmetic.
> This is Mr Grant. He has a good sense of humour and can make us laugh when we feel downhearted.

Prepare a board with the heading 'Gifts we have to offer', or make a 'gift tag tree' by planting a bare branch in a pot. Provide small pieces of paper ('gift tags') and pencils so that children can write down either their affirmations of others or their offers of help. These will be pinned on the board or tied on to the tree.

Assembly

1. Talk about how the school is made up of many people of different ages, sizes and personalities. Discuss with the children how everyone has something which is their special gift or ability to offer to the community.
2. Invite the children to take a moment to think quietly of someone in their class who is particularly good at something. Ask the children/teachers who are nominating others to introduce their nomination and describe that person's gift. Some nominees could perhaps show a painting, do some quick maths or play a short piece of music, as appropriate.
3. Write the brief descriptions on the 'gift tags' and either pin them to the board or tie them on to the tree.
4. Introduce the idea of using your gifts to help others. Help the children to feel confident about offering to share their gifts (e.g. Sam is ready to teach football skills. Anne will help Year 1 with skipping). Take time to celebrate the range of gifts and the importance of every type of ability (e.g. being a peacemaker is as important as writing well).

    Point out to the children the importance of recognizing and encouraging each other's gifts and also recognizing and improving our own abilities. Discuss the importance of sharing our gifts with the community by teaching each other.

    Show the 'Gifts we have to offer' board or tree or gift tag tree and encourage the children to use the board or tree to affirm each other or offer help to each other during the week.

Time for reflection

In a moment of quiet, invite the children to think of the gifts they have and how they can improve these and share them with others. Invite the children to be aware of the gifts of others and how they can encourage and celebrate each other's achievements.

Songs

'The wise may bring their learning' (*Come and Praise*, 64)
'The best gift' (*Come and Praise*, 59)

Curriculum links

- Literacy: Read *The Clown of God*, by Tomie de Paola (Harcourt, ISBN 0156181924).
- PSHE: Use circle time for an affirmation exercise, e.g. 'Pat on the back': everyone thinks of something affirmative to say about the person next to them and then gives them a pat on the back. Help the children to develop skills in self-evaluation by discussing their gifts and which aspects they need to develop.
- Art/Music: Help the children to identify particular gifts or techniques of artists and musicians.
- Local history: Help the children to discover if people with particular gifts have lived in their town or area, e.g. inventors, politicians. Explore whether artists, potters or writers live locally today, and if possible arrange a visit to talk about their gifts.

FAMILIES

By Kate Fleming

Suitable for Whole School

Aim

To explore the diversity of the family unit. To encourage harmony and the need for understanding within families.

Preparation and materials

- A pack of Happy Families cards – or a sample family from the game drawn by children in advance.
- Four Year 6 children rehearsed in advance to present the play script (optional).

Assembly

1. Introduce and talk about the game of Happy Families, asking if any children know the game. Explain how it works and then introduce the drama. Or go through the families on the cards (or the sample family), drawing out the point that every family in the game has the same number of adults and children.

    Four Year 6 children are sitting round a table playing Happy Families.

    Child 1 Have you got Master Chips the Carpenter's son?
    Child 3 Yes! (*hands card over*)
    Child 1 Thank you. Excellent! That means I've got the whole family: Mr Chips the Carpenter, Mrs Chips the Carpenter's wife, Miss Chips the Carpenter's daughter, AND NOW – Master Chips the Carpenter's son! A complete family! (*spreads cards down on table*)

Child 2 Have you got Miss Bun the Baker's daughter?
Child 4 No.
Child 2 Oh no! I need her really badly.
Child 3 Have you got Mrs Bun the Baker's wife?
Child 2 Yes. (*hands card over*)
Child 3 Have you got Mr Bun the Baker?
Child 2 Yes. (*hands card over reluctantly*)
Child 3 Now I've got the complete Bun family. (*spreads cards out on the table*)
Child 4 Have you got Mr Pots the Painter?
Child 1 Yes. (*hands card over*)
Child 4 May I present the Pots family: Mr Pots the Painter, Mrs Pots the Painter's wife, Miss Pots the Painter's daughter, and finally Master Pots the Painter's son.
Child 1 It's funny how all these families in this game are the same. My family isn't like that, it's just me, my mum and my sister Susie.
Child 2 My family is not like yours or the game. It's my dad and me.
Child 3 My gran lives with us, so my family is me, Mum and Dad, Tom, Sean and Gran.
Child 4 There are seven of us, Mum, Dad, Jenny and Jeff, my stepsister and brother, Phoebe, Paul and me.

2. If you have used the drama, explain that these children have found that real families come in all shapes and sizes. They are not all the same like this game of Happy Families. Talk about the fact that all our families are made up in different ways, each family, like each person, is special – unique.

3. Ask the children to put up their hand to answer the following questions.

   Who is a son?
   Who is a daughter?
   Who is a nephew?
   Who is a niece?
   Who is a cousin?

So if you are sons, daughters, nephews, nieces and cousins, others will be mothers, fathers, uncles, aunties, grannies and granddads.

Time for reflection

Belonging to a family is important.
Lions belong to the cat family.
Dogs belong to the canine family.
Cats belong to the feline family.
Rats are all rodents.
And we belong to our own special families,
which all belong to the world-wide family of humankind.

We need to value our families,
however they are made up,
big or small, near to us or far away.
Let's enjoy the feeling of belonging,
and be thankful that families can be so varied
and that each family is special.

God bless all those that I love.
God bless all those that love me.
God bless all those that love those that I love
And all those that love those that love me.
Amen.

Song

'I belong to a family, the biggest on earth' (*Come and Praise*, 69)

PRAYER
By Jill Fuller

Suitable for Whole School

Aim

To think about different forms of prayer. To help children understand that prayer is a part of all major faiths and was an important part of the life of Jesus. To help them to be comfortable with both stillness and silence as ways of prayer.

Preparation and materials

- Make a display which can act as a focus for the worship. It could include some of the following: candle, cross, bowl of flowers, icon, rosary, prayer mat, prayer wheel, stone.

Assembly

1. Introduce the concept of prayer with some basic explanation. Prayer is part of all major faiths. Talk about how every person who prays does so in their own way. People sometimes go to special places to pray: church, synagogue, mosque. Discuss how some people find it easier to pray in the open, when they are walking, or sitting in a quiet place.
   Some people use special aids to help them to concentrate. Show the items from the display, e.g. using a prayer mat or a prayer wheel, a rosary or holding a special object like a stone. Some people like to focus on a candle, a cross, an icon or some beautiful flowers. Some people take up a special position to pray, like kneeling, meditation poses, etc.
2. Point out that Jesus took time to pray and thought that prayer was important. Read Luke 5.16: Jesus 'would go away to lonely places, where he prayed'. See also Mark 1.35: 'He went out of the town to a lonely place, where he prayed', and

Matthew 14.22–23: 'Then Jesus made the disciples get into the boat and go on ahead to the other side of the lake, while he sent the people away. After sending the people away, he went up a hill by himself to pray.'

3. If appropriate, you could remind the children of other times when Jesus prayed, and point out that they included all kinds of moods and occasions: times when he was happy, thankful, sad, tired, confused or frightened. Matthew 19.13: Jesus blesses the children with prayer; Mark 6.41: Jesus gives thanks before the feeding of the 5,000; Mark 14.32–36: Jesus prays to God in the garden of Gethsemane.

    Explain that Christians believe in a loving God who wants to share all our hopes and fears and that prayer is a way of sharing our lives with God. Prayer can be a time when we give thanks, say we are sorry, or ask for help. Point out that even people who do not believe in a God often find it helpful to be still and silent, just to think.

4. Read the following poem and ask the children to think about it – how would they answer the questions?

    Is that praying?
    by Gordon Lamont

    I'm running a race and I want to be first.
    'Please God, let me win,'
    I say – but do I pray?
    Is that praying?

    I'm playing with my friends
    and everything's fine.
    I lose track of time.
    'I'm glad to be alive today,' I say
    to no one in particular.
    Is that praying?

    Things have gone wrong
    an argument – a fight.
    I couldn't sleep at all last night.
    Dear God, please put things right.
    Is that praying?

Time for reflection

Ask the children to make themselves comfortable so that they can be very still. They should decide whether they want to close their eyes or focus on something in the display. Ask them to take the next minute to reflect on and remember the presence of God, or think about the day ahead.

Dear God,
Thank you that we can always talk to you:
whoever we are,
wherever we are,
whatever we feel.

Thank you that you hear what we say,
and what we do not say.
You know what we mean
even when we don't know ourselves.
Amen.

Songs

'Shalom' (*Come and Praise 2*, 141)
'Be still and know that I am God' (Taizé chant)
'Be still and know that I am God' (from *There is One Among Us: Shorter Songs for Worship*, John Bell, Wild Goose Publications ISBN 1901557103)

Curriculum links

- RE: Look at different ways of praying in different faiths.
- History: Find a prayer from the particular period being studied, e.g. a Celtic prayer, a Collect from Cranmer's Book of Common Prayer, a Victorian prayer.
- Music: Look at hymn writing as prayer in song.

ALL TOGETHER NOW! – THE EXPRESSIVE ARTS
By Gill Hartley

Suitable for Whole School

Aim

To celebrate the joys of singing, dancing and acting together.

Preparation and materials

- A CD or cassette of disco music.

Assembly

1. Sing the school's favourite assembly song. It can be on any theme, but aim to encourage the children to enjoy it as they sing!
2. Ask the children how they felt singing together. Would it have been the same if they had sung it on their own?
3. Play some disco music. Ask the children to tell you what is good about dancing at a disco. Ask them what the difference is between dancing at a disco and dancing to the music on their own.
4. Ask if there are any children who do other sorts of dancing, e.g. ballet, country dancing, line dancing. Encourage them to tell you about their enjoyment of it.
5. Ask the children to think back to the last school play/concert/ performance (as appropriate). Ask any who were involved to tell you what they liked about it. Again ask what the difference is between doing something like that on your own and taking part with other people. In all of these discussions, aim to draw out the fun and enjoyment in singing, dancing or acting with other people.

6. Make the point that everyone involved contributes to the success of a concert or play, from the people who work backstage or on costumes to the people at the door, to the performers themselves – not forgetting the audience, whose role is vital!

Time for reflection

Ask the children to join in with the 'thank you' responses in this prayer.

> Dear God,
> For the fun of singing songs together:
> **Thank you!**
> For sad music, happy music and music that makes us laugh:
> **Thank you!**
> For stereos and CD players that mean we can listen to music at any time:
> **Thank you!**
> For the joy of dancing:
> **Thank you!**
> For those times when it feels really good to turn the music up loud and dance till we drop:
> **Thank you!**
> For all the times when we have enjoyed acting in plays and performing in concerts:
> **Thank you!**
> Thank you for all the fun of singing and dancing and acting.
> **Amen.**

Song

'Praise the Lord in the rhythm of your music' (*Come and Praise*, 33)

WINTER

By Kate Fleming

Suitable for Whole School
(Note the option for KS2b children at 7. below)

Aim

To think about the beauty and the magic of winter. To acknowledge that while some people love wintertime there are others who dread it.

Preparation and materials

- Dress up for the assembly in scarf, gloves, woolly hat and coat.
- This assembly includes as an option a sound picture of a storm. This could be a 'live' event involving the whole school, or one class could prepare it in advance for the rest to listen to.
- Introductory music: 'Winter' from Vivaldi's *Four Seasons*.

Assembly

1. Ask the children about the clothes you are wearing. How are they different from the sort of thing you might wear on your summer holiday?
2. Ask the children how they keep warm in the winter – warm clothes, central heating, roaring fire, hot water bottles, hot drinks.
3. Look at the contrast between inside warm houses, with people snuggling up in cosy beds and outside, where the cold wind whistles round chimney pots, ponds freeze over, cars in the street are covered in frost. Then just before the dawn the snow begins to fall, lightly at first and then more and more heavily as it settles gently on the sleeping landscape.
4. Introduce and conduct the children in a sound picture of a windy, stormy night. Some make the sounds of a hurricane

wind, others the sound of heavy rain, others pretend to be shivering people, and so on.

5. Ask the children to think about when it snows. Ask them if they are able to tell, even before they draw the curtains back, that it has been snowing during the night. Is the light different through the curtains? Is it unusually quiet? And when you open the curtains, as if by magic everything – your house, your garden, your street, your car, and as far as you can see – has been transformed into a different place, a wondrous and exciting place. You simply can't stop looking at it. You dash downstairs and put on your scarf, gloves, woolly hat and coat and rush outside to welcome the winter snow.

6. Ask for suggestions of the different ways the children play in the snow: snowballing, building snowmen, sliding, making footprints, tobogganing. They probably find the snow brilliantly exciting and fun, but does everyone feel the same way about it?

    Think whether for some people the snow might be unwelcome. Who might they be? Older people who cannot get around as easily as they once did. People who have difficulty travelling to work. Farmers getting food to their animals and shepherds looking after new-born lambs. Disabled people, for instance those in wheelchairs.

    So while we are having a great time playing in the snow, perhaps we should remember that there are some people who long for the spring, and the warmth of the sun when Mother Earth will wake up from her long, cold sleep and start again.

7. Read one of these two poems. The first is suitable for the whole school, the second, from Shakespeare's *Love's Labour's Lost*, is difficult but might be suitable for some KS2 children and could be used as the basis for further work on literacy.

>   1
>   The North wind doth blow
>   And we shall have snow
>   And what will the robin
>   Do then? Poor thing.
>   He'll sit in the barn
>   And keep himself warm

And hide his head under his wing.
Poor thing.

2
When icicles hang by the wall,
And Dick the shepherd blows his nail,
And Tom bears logs into the hall,
And milk comes frozen home in pail,
When blood is nipp'd and ways be foul,
Then nightly sings the staring owl, Tu-who;
Tu-whit, Tu-who – a merry note,
While greasy Joan doth keel the pot.

When all aloud the wind doth blow,
And coughing drowns the parson's saw,
And birds sit brooding in the snow,
And Marian's nose looks red and raw,
When roasted crabs hiss in the bowl,
Then nightly sings the staring owl, Tu-who;
Tu-whit, Tu-who – a merry note,
While greasy Joan doth keel the pot.

That was written a long time ago by William Shakespeare. When you go back to the classroom you could see if you could find out if winter has changed since Shakespeare's time.

Time for reflection

Dear God,
Thank you for the gift of winter,
the wonder of the snow, and the beauty of frost.
Help us to appreciate this important season
and help us to remember that for some people it can be a hardship.
Amen.

Song

'Lay my white cloak on the ground' (*Come and Praise 2*, 112)

Curriculum links

Science, PSHE, English

NO ROOM . . .

By Gordon and Ronni Lamont

Suitable for Whole School

Aim

A dramatic retelling of the Nativity, involving the whole school, that can be used to focus on the Bible story and meaning of Christmas and/or the issue of homelessness.

Preparation and materials

- Ensure that you are familiar with the Nativity story and the children's action that accompanies each part.
- Choose the reflection(s) you wish to use. Ask one or two children to read the reflection(s), if appropriate.

Assembly

1. Explain that in this morning's assembly, the whole school is going to tell the story of the first Christmas. Everyone will have a part and will need to join in.
2. Begin with the story of the census. Explain what a census is – an official counting and collection of everyone's details – and say that you will have a quick census now. You will count to three, and everyone in the hall must clearly say their name and their age: 1, 2, 3.
   Obviously a real census couldn't work like that. Everyone would need to give his or her details one at a time, and this could be a very long process. Mary and Joseph went to Bethlehem because Joseph was a descendant of King David, and that was where he had to give his details.
3. Explain that they had a long and tiring journey and this was especially difficult for Mary because she was soon to have a baby. Ask the children to stand up, and walk on the spot.

They are getting more and more tired, hungry and thirsty. But, no matter how tired they are, they just have to keep going until, at last, they arrive in Bethlehem. Now at last they can sit down, with a sigh because they're so tired.

If appropriate and if time allows, ask a few children to the front to share their mimes.

4. Explain that Bethlehem was full to bursting point with people arriving for the census, and all the inns were very busy. Ask the children to think about the kinds of things that would be going on in the inns. Food being made, drinks being served, guests being welcomed, beds being made up, and so on. On the count of three, ask the children to act out the busyness of Bethlehem where they're sitting: 1, 2, 3.

If appropriate and if time allows, ask a few children to the front to share their mimes.

5. Mary and Joseph, tired as they are, have to look for a room for the night. They knock on lots of doors. Ask the children to demonstrate door knocking, either on the floor, or by clapping. Practise until everyone has a clear 1, 2, 3 rhythm, or a more complicated one if you wish!

Mary and Joseph knock at the first inn (*children knock*) – no room. They knock at the second inn (*children knock*) – no room. They knock at the third inn (*children knock*) – no room. They are about to give up, but they knock at one more inn (*children knock*) – no room . . . unless they would like to sleep in the stable with the animals. Sorry, but that's the only space left.

6. So Mary and Joseph spend the night in the stable and that's where the baby is born. Ask the children to imagine that they are holding a new-born baby, being very careful as they gently rock him.

If appropriate and if time allows, ask a few children to the front to share their mimes.

Alternatively, practise and perform a shout of joy at the baby's birth: Three cheers for the new baby, hip, hip hooray!

Time for reflection

Ask the children to imagine that they are still holding the baby, as you or individual children read one or more of the following.

1
New life, new light – a baby is born.
New hope, this night – a baby is born.
New thanks we say – a baby is born.
News thanks this day – a baby is born.
Who will he be – this baby so small?
What things will he see – this baby so small?
What will happen to him – this baby so small?
What changes will he bring – this baby so small?

2
We think of Mary and Joseph alone in a strange town.
They had nowhere to live, no one to turn to.
They were hungry and cold, perhaps a little afraid.
They needed shelter, somewhere to sleep –
Somewhere for Mary to have her baby.

We think of people today, alone in strange towns and cities.
People who have nowhere to live, no one to turn to.
People who are hungry and cold, perhaps a little afraid.
They need shelter, somewhere to sleep –
Somewhere to call home.

Dear God,
We say thank you for our homes.
We pray for homeless people all over the world.
Help us in this country to do all we can to bring an end to homelessness.
Amen.

3
Dear God,
We thank you that Jesus was born.
We thank you that he grew up to teach us about God's love.
We think of such a special baby being born,
Not in a palace
Not in a rich house
Not in a house at all
But in a stable with the animals.

Thank you for Jesus,
A special friend for all people.
Amen.

🎵 Song

'Peace, perfect peace' (*Come and Praise*, 53)

Curriculum links

PSHE, RE

THE COOK'S TALE
By Kate Fleming

Suitable for KS2b

Aim

To look at the story of the three Wise Men from a different perspective. To think imaginatively about hidden characters in stories. To highlight the importance of love in a materialist world.

Preparation and materials

None.

Assembly

1. Ask the children: Who has had a new baby born into their family? Ask about visitors who have come to see the new baby with presents and cards. People who live nearby and people from a long way away.

    Explain that this happened when Jesus was born too. His family had visitors – shepherds from nearby and three men from far away. Three men who went on a long journey to see Jesus and bring him presents. Who were they? Yes, the three Wise Men. They travelled for many days riding on camels through difficult and dangerous countryside.

    Do you think they did this amazing journey on their own? Just the three of them? Well, they didn't. They had people who worked for them to help. They took people to carry the luggage, people to look after the camels, people to protect them from robbers, people to advise them, and people to cook for them.

2. Explain that we don't know anything about the servants, but here's an imaginary story about one of them. In charge of the

cooks was Awad, and it is his story that I am going to tell you this morning.

The Cook's Tale

Awad had worked as a cook in Lord Melchior's grand palace since he was a boy. He was now head chef and extremely proud of his position. The food he cooked was famous throughout the land and his services were much sought after. One morning in December excitement spread though the palace like wildfire, arriving at the kitchens just as Awad was preparing a particularly tasty falafel for Lord Melchior and his special guests for that evening, Lord Casper and Lord Balthasar.

For two days and nights, these astrologers had been shut up in their observatory studying the rising of a new star that had appeared in the sky. It was bright, so bright that it stood out from the other stars like a powerful king would stand out in a crowd.

Now the news was out. The lords, Melchior, Casper and Balthasar, were to follow that star to find the new-born baby who was to be a very special King. 'It was written by the prophets,' Awad's kitchen-hand Cesar told him. 'They are going after dinner tonight, and WE are going with them!'

Awad was excited – he had never been away from home before, but he was anxious as well. What food would he take? How would he cook all the special dishes that the great lords so admired? How would they carry the olive oil, the honey, the game, geese, fish, birds' eggs, not to mention the wine?

Poor Awad was in such a panic, rushing round the kitchen checking, counting, shouting, indeed close to tears, when his beloved master Lord Melchior swept in. 'Awad, why the worry?' he said in his deep, gentle voice. 'All we require is your skill as a cook, your secret herbs and spices, and the rest we will find on the way. Awad, we are going to worship the newly-born King who has been heralded by a magnificent new star. That alone will feed us.'

Awad felt a deep calm sweep over him. He felt valued and special, and he knew that this was to be the journey of his lifetime.

Awad packed his cooking knives, his mother's pestle and

mortar, and his two favourite pots, into which he stowed cumin, fenugreek, dill, sesame and mustard seeds, hyssop, aniseed, mint, sage, marjoram, bay leaves, coriander, caraway and saffron. With these he was confident he could cook anything for the great men of the stars.

The journey was hard: the wrong time of the year, cold and wet underfoot. They did find food on the way, some growing wild and some purchased from shepherds and goatherds. Simple but delicious fare, cooked over open fires under the night sky with the new star always there beckoning them on towards Jerusalem. Then they came into warmer weather and Awad and Cesar were able to pick fresh pomegranates from the trees, pistachio nuts, grapes from wild vines and juicy melons ripened by the midday sun.

Jerusalem was a welcome sight and King Herod a magnificent host. There were barrels of wine, a roasted ox and all manner of sumptuous food for all to feast on, but no sign of the baby. The travellers were surprised to learn that it was thought he was to be born in Bethlehem, further west. 'Find him,' Herod commanded, 'so that I too can worship the new King.' But his voice trembled, his face was white and his eyes cruel were and full of hatred.

The party was over.

When the lords and their servants arrived in Bethlehem the star seemed to stop over a humble home. Lord Melchior, Lord Casper and Lord Balthasar dismounted their camels and entered. They presented their gifts of gold, frankincense and myrrh.

Awad gazed in wonder at the newly-born King. He felt a warm hand on his shoulder and looked up into the wise eyes of his master Lord Melchior. 'Well, Awad, my dear friend, what are you thinking? How do you feel? No roast goose, spitted quails or fatted ox here!'

'No, my Lord,' said Awad. 'Simple herbs here, but mixed with another essential ingredient.' The great lord swung round, taking Awad with him, and whispered in his ear. 'Better a dinner of herbs where love is, than a fatted ox and hatred with it.'

Departure from Bethlehem was immediate. Back east to their own country, using a different route.

3. Ask the children: Why do you think the lords decided to take a different route back to their own country? What do you think Lord Melchior meant when he whispered to Awad, 'Better a dinner of herbs where love is, than a fatted ox and hatred with it'? Do you think it has anything to do with Awad's 'essential ingredient' that he had felt in the presence of the baby?

Time for reflection

Dear God,
The three Wise Men journeyed from their grand palaces to the humble stable in Bethlehem
and experienced the importance of love.
Help us to learn from this and make love our essential ingredient.
Amen.

Songs

'As with gladness men of old' (*Hymns Ancient and Modern*, 79)
'Riding out across the desert' (*Come and Praise*, 124)

Curriculum links

English, RE, PSHE

Spring Term

EPIPHANY

By Gordon and Ronni Lamont

Suitable for Whole School

Aim

To tell the story of the Wise Visitors to the baby Jesus (Matthew 2.1–12). To explore the notion of finding God, transforming everyday events into something special.

Preparation and materials

- You will need to know your 'script' so that you can direct the action of the story. The children involved will be responding to your instructions – they do not need to prepare in advance. The Head or other member of staff is required to play Herod.
- You will need three cardboard crowns and three gifts – either richly decorated boxes for the traditional gifts, or boxes covered with white paper representing up-to-date gifts (see 2. below).

Assembly

1. Ask if anyone can tell you anything about the story in the Bible when some Wise Visitors (Wise Men, or Kings) came from the East to visit the baby Jesus. Collect together the children's ideas and make the point that the Bible does not say how many of these Wise Visitors there were, but it is a tradition to say that there were three. Ask for three volunteers to play the parts of the visitors. Give them each a crown.
2. Talk about the gifts that they brought. The Bible tells us that these were expensive and valuable items of the time. Gold – a precious metal; frankincense and myrrh – expensive perfumes and ointments. Show the decorated boxes to represent each gift.

Alternatively, ask the children what three gifts might be given today – valuable and important things from our time. Perhaps gold, maybe a Playstation, a collection of books? If you take this option, use boxes covered with white paper to represent the gifts and write or draw the articles on them. Ask for three volunteers to be servants and give each a gift to carry.

3. Now tell the story based on Matthew 2.1–12, with the children miming the actions as you speak. Start with the Wise Ones looking up at the sky and the servants asleep on the ground.

The Wise Ones see a special star in the sky (*Wise Ones look up and point*). They talk together about what this might mean (*they huddle*).

They decide that they must go on a journey to greet a great new king. So they wake their servants, collect together provisions for a long journey and set off (*they mime preparations*).

It is a very long way. (*Lead the party around the hall, adding the following at various points*) Sometimes they are freezing cold (*all mime shivering*). Sometimes it is very hot (*all mime walking in great heat*).

They are very tired and long to stop (*mime tiredness*), but the star keeps leading them onwards (*Wise Ones point to star and urge party to keep moving*).

As they come near to their journey's end, King Herod gets to hear of them and summons them to him (*Herod beckons them over. The servants hold back, the Wise Ones bow to Herod*).

Herod is very interested in this talk of a new king. Perhaps the travellers would be good enough to call back when they have found him so that Herod can worship him too (*Wise Ones and Herod mime regal conversation*).

4. Stop the narrative here and discuss with all the children what they think Herod may be thinking about. Draw out the idea that he really wants to do away with this new King, who he sees as an enemy, or rival.

5. Continue the story:

   At last the wandering star leads them all to the place where the new King is. The Wise Ones go in and kneel before the baby (*Wise Ones kneel*), while the servants peep in from outside (*servants peep and try to see*). The Wise Ones give their gifts to the baby's mother (*Wise Ones put down gifts*).

6. Does anyone know who the baby was that they saw? Explain that this was Jesus, who would grow up to be a very different kind of king from King Herod.

7. Continue the story:

   Finally, after their long journey and exciting day, the Wise Ones go to sleep (*they all lie down on the floor*). As they sleep, they have a dream. In the dream God tells them not to go back to Herod, but to go home a different way.

   So the next morning, they quickly get up, pack their bags and set off for home (*all mime packing and starting journey*) but by a different road (*guide them on a different route around the hall back to their starting point*).

   Herod is very cross indeed when he realizes that he's been tricked (*teacher playing Herod stands up and walks out angrily*).

8. Ask the mimers to sit down. Explain that the Wise Ones found something very special at the end of their long journey, and we're going to think about that now.

Time for reflection

The Wise Ones went on a long journey to find a special person.
Think about the special people in your life.
Who is really special to you?

Herod was jealous of the new baby.
He lied to the Wise Ones, pretending that he wanted to worship Jesus.
Think about what makes you jealous.
Are there things that other people have that you wish were yours?
Do you ever tell lies to get your own way?

The Wise Ones found what they were looking for, by following a star.
Think about what you would like to do today.
How will you make it happen?

Song

'Travel on' (*Come and Praise*, 42)

Curriculum link

PSHE

WOLFGANG AMADEUS MOZART – NEVER A DULL MOMENT!

By Margaret Liversidge

Suitable for KS1

Aim

To enable young children to see that their liveliness is a valuable part of learning and growing.

Preparation and materials

- A board or card showing the words 'Wolfgang Amadeus Mozart 1756–1791'.
- Cards for three individual children to hold showing the numbers 4, 5 and 6 written large.
- Introductory music by Mozart, e.g. *Minuet in G*.

Assembly

1. Ask the children to tell you about some of the thoughts they may have had while waiting for the assembly to begin. Prompt with some suggestions, e.g. about friends, playtime, recent classroom activity, etc. Explain that the human brain is rather like a computer, able to take in and sort out information all the time, and this is part of how we learn things.
2. Ask them to list some of the physical activities they enjoy doing. Encourage generalizations such as running, skipping, hopping as well as more specific sports such as football and gymnastics. Explain that, like the brain, our bodies are also constantly active and this is how we learn and grow.
3. Explain that you are going to tell the children about a boy just like them who was very lively and had difficulty sitting still.

Say his name together from the board. Mozart was Austrian, born in Salzburg.

4. Tell the story of Mozart as follows:

> Once there was a boy who couldn't sit still at all. He couldn't stop thinking either, and what he thought about most of the time was music. He made up tunes in his head all day long and even during the night! Mozart was full of fun and he was always singing and jumping about and amusing other people. His parents realized that his tunes were rather clever and so they decided to help him with his music.
>
> (*Child holds up card 4*) When Mozart was only 4 years old he started to have proper music lessons, along with his sister.
>
> (*Child holds up card 5*) When he was only 5 years old, he was so good at playing the piano that his parents took him on tour to other countries to show off his talent.
>
> (*Child holds up card 6*) When he was only 6 years old he started to write down his music on paper using musical notes so that other people could play the tunes he was making up in his head. His first special written tune was called *Minuet in G*. If you used introductory music, explain that Mozart composed the music they heard.

5. Remind them that Mozart was a child like them. Draw the application that the ideas in each child's busy mind and the things they enjoy doing are to be encouraged as they learn to realize what they are especially good at.

Time for reflection

Tell the children that we are going to thank God for our clever minds and busy bodies. Possibly allow a quiet moment during which the children are guided to reflect on their favourite activities.

> Thank you God for our clever minds.
> Help us to learn well.
> Thank you God for our busy bodies.
> Help us to keep fit.
> **Amen.**

🎵 Song

'You shall go out with joy' (*Come and Praise 2*, 98)

Optional rhyme

> I wiggle my fingers,
> I wiggle my toes,
> I wiggle my eyebrows,
> I wiggle my nose!
> Now no more wiggles are left in me,
> and I'm as still . . . as still . . . can be.

The rhyme can be ended with a surprise action or noise, which takes the children unawares and changes the mood. They will easily and quickly respond to a repeat of the rhyme which, this time, could maintain the stillness.

Curriculum links

Music, PSHE, PE

WHY WORRY? (1)

By Kate Fleming

Suitable for Whole School

Note: There are two free-standing assemblies on the same theme. Either can be used independently or they can be used one after the other.

Aim

To explore worrying and look at reasons and remedies for it.

Preparation and materials

None.

Assembly

1. Tell the children that the assembly will start with a guessing game. They should raise their hands when all the clues have been read out if they know the answer.

   What am I?
   I like stinging nettles.
   My cousins like cabbages,
   lady's smock or garlic mustard.
   We all like buddleias.
   I start life as an egg,
   then I change, then change again,
   before I change into a beautiful
   Peacock, Red Admiral, Orange Tip,
   Common Blue, Cabbage White . . .
   What am I?

   Answer: A butterfly.

2. Let's look at the word butterfly. If you change round the two sounds, butterfly becomes flutterby. Some people nickname butterflies flutterbies. Why do you think that is? Fragile wings that flutter.

3. Ask the younger children to show how their fingers can flutter. Ask them to place one fluttering hand into their other still hand. Demonstrate this for them. What does it feel like?
4. Sometimes we admit to having butterflies in our tummies. What does this mean? Usually that we are anxious, nervous, worried about something. Ask the children what kinds of things they worry about. Monsters, darkness, being late for school, not having the right clothes on, getting lost, witches, dragons . . .
5. Point out the difference between worrying about real things and worrying about imaginary things; worrying about what we know *will* happen and what we think *might* happen. Take examples of different types of worry from the children's suggestions above.
6. Ask the children what usually makes worries disappear. Talking about them to parents and carers, grandparents, friends, teachers. Worries don't like being talked about, because when they are talked about, they become NO WORRIES.

Time for reflection

Dear God,
When I have a worry,
be it big or small,
give me someone to talk to
so that together we can work out the reason for the worry,
and how I can make it go away.
Amen.

Song

'When night arrives' (*Come and Praise* 2, 92)

Curriculum links

English, PSHE

WHY WORRY? (2)

By Kate Fleming

Suitable for KS2

Note: There are two free-standing assemblies on the same theme. Either can be used independently or they can be used one after the other.

Aim

To explore the positive and negative outcomes of worrying.

Preparation and materials

- Rehearse scripts 1 and 2 with four older children in advance, or improvise dramas around the themes in class and develop them for performance in the assembly.
- Introductory music: 'Why Worry?' from the Dire Straits album *Brothers in Arms*.

Assembly

Introduce the two dramas. Ask the children to listen carefully to what you are about to say and to think about the words as they watch the dramas, which are two different examples of worrying situations.

> Sometimes we worry about real things and sometimes our worries are imaginary.
> Sometimes worrying can be important and sometimes it is unimportant.
> Sometimes it can be constructive and sometimes it can be destructive.
> Sometimes it can lead to positive results, sometimes to negative ones.

Ask the children if they can work out which situation has a positive result and which a negative one.

Script 1

Emma and Kylie are sitting at a table with their lunch boxes. They open their boxes.

Emma   Good, you've got crisps, Kylie, can we share?
Kylie   Yes.
Emma   What kind of sandwiches have you got?
Kylie   Cheese and tomato. They're really good. What have you got in yours?
Emma   Cold sausage and HP sauce, which are my most favourite sandwiches in the whole world, and a bar of chocolate too! Mum must have cooked these sausages especially for me, because we didn't have sausages last night for tea. In a way, that makes it worse.
Kylie   What do you mean? What does it make worse?
Emma   I was really horrid to Mum last night. I stormed off to my room and slammed the door so hard that my Backstreet Boys photo fell off the windowsill. I can still hear the noise of the door slamming. I know Mum was upset by the look in her eyes. The thing is, it's still playing on my mind. Mum had gone to work by the time I came down to breakfast this morning and Dad hardly said a word.
Kylie   Are you still worried?
Emma   Yes. It won't go away. So I've decided to say I'm sorry as soon as I get home. I think I'll make her a special card – she'll like that.

Exit with lunch boxes.

Script 2

Ed and Billy are changing for football.

Ed   Come on, Billy, hurry up. We'll be late for football and old Barnsey will go berserk. What's the matter with you? Why is it taking you so long to get your boots on? You're not David Beckham you know!
Billy   I'm tired, Ed, I didn't sleep very well last night. I lay awake worrying that something was under my bed.
Ed   The only thing under your bed is a mess.
Billy   No, listen! I could hear a scratching, snuffling noise and

	I was sure that some slimy monster was waiting there, just ready to slither up on my bed and crush me to death with its deadly poisonous tentacles.
Ed	Sounds like my sister.
Billy	It's not funny, you know! Then at last I fell asleep and everything was fine this morning. No monsters, no nothing. The scratching, snuffling noise turned out to be simply the wind brushing the tree against my window!
Ed	You're such a wimp, Billy. Fancy wasting all that time worrying about nothing at all. I think you watch too many horror films.
Billy	You sound just like my dad.
Ed	Come on, Becks. See if you can find the back of the net for a change.

Run off with football.

Ask the children which of the two worries was completely unnecessary, and which was more 'real'.

> Sometimes we worry about real things and sometimes our worries are imaginary.
> Sometimes worrying can be important and sometimes it is unimportant.
> Sometimes it can be constructive and sometimes it can be destructive.
> Sometimes it can lead to positive results, sometimes to negative ones.

Stress the importance of talking about worries. In these dramas Emma could talk to Kylie and Billy to Ed.

Time for reflection

This is a short, old prayer that helps us to put worries in their proper place.

> God grant me the serenity to accept the things I cannot change,
> the courage to change the things I can,
> and the wisdom to know the difference.
> **Amen.**

Songs

'Journey of life' (*Come and Praise*, 45)
'He gave me eyes so I could see' (*Come and Praise*, 18)

Curriculum links

English, PSHE

THE BIBLE
By Gill Hartley

Suitable for Whole School

Aim

To begin to appreciate the variety and inspiration of the Bible.

Preparation and materials

- A Bible, preferably a good modern translation or children's Bible, in a pocket/handbag/briefcase/shopping bag.
- Organize the children from two classes to bring in one book each (on any subject), and bring in some spares yourself, to make up a total of 66 books.

Assembly

1. Ask the children to bring out the books they have brought in and to pile them up one by one. Suggest that the rest of the school counts the books out loud as they are piled up.
2. When you have counted up to the total of 66, ask the children if they would like to carry all those books at once. Tell the children that you have 66 books in your pocket/handbag/briefcase/shopping bag! Bring out the Bible and explain that it is not just one book, but 66! Ask if they know any of the titles of the individual books of the Bible. Among the answers you may receive are: Matthew, Mark, Luke, John (the Gospels); Psalms; Genesis.
3. Use any answers you receive to demonstrate the different sorts of books in the Bible, e.g.:

    Matthew, Mark, Luke, John (the Gospels) – stories about Jesus' life (i.e. biography).
    Psalms – a book of poetry or songs.
    Genesis – stories about God's people long ago (i.e. legends, myths and history).

You might also want to talk about other sorts of books in the Bible, such as:

> Proverbs – a book of wise sayings and mottoes.
> Acts of the Apostles – stories about the first followers of Jesus (i.e. history).
> The Epistles (e.g. Romans, Corinthians, Ephesians) – letters written to the first Christian churches.

4. Illustrate some of the different sorts of literature to be found in the Bible by reading some extracts from a good modern translation or children's Bible, such as one of the stories of Jesus' birth (e.g. Matthew 2 or Luke 2), a poem or song (e.g. Psalm 23) or the beginning of the story of Noah (e.g. Genesis 6.9 onwards).
5. If appropriate, explore with the children the division of the Bible into two sections: the Old Testament, which describes the time before Jesus was born, and the New Testament, which tells the story of Jesus and what his followers did after he died.
6. Ask the children what this collection of books called the Bible is for. After considering whatever answers you receive, explain that the Bible as a whole is considered a special book by Christians. Many people believe that God inspired all its different authors to write it to teach them what God is like. Explain that other religions also use the Bible – the Old Testament is the special book of the Jewish people, and Muslims find the stories of Jesus helpful, for example.

Time for reflection

Dear God,
Thank you for all kinds of books:
for books that are fun to read,
for books that help us in our lessons,
and for books that teach us things we did not know.
Thank you for all the people who have written books which help others to learn.
Thank you for the Bible which has taught so many people about God.
Help us to respect the books that are important to other people.
Amen.

Song

'The ink is black' (*Come and Praise*, 67)

MUMS

By Gordon and Ronni Lamont

Suitable for KS2

Aim

To contrast life in the West with life in parts of the developing world, using the experience of mothers as an example.

Preparation and materials

- You will need to rehearse three good speakers for the poem and you could expand the material by adding simple mime or still pictures.

Assembly

1. Introduce the theme of the assembly – thinking about mothers in different parts of the world. Discuss any recent news stories about the developing world that the children may know of.
2. Introduce the poem.

    ONE
    I'm number one, a very busy mum.
    I have so much to do looking after everyone.
    Jobs in the home,
    jobs outside.
    People want me all the time,
    but I take it in my stride.
    I'm number one – a very busy mum.

    TWO
    I'm number two, I'm waiting in the queue.
    I'm at the water well you see, then there are beans to stew.
    I'll walk two miles back,
    with water on my head.

I make this journey twice each day.
I'd love a tap instead.
I'm number two, I'm waiting in the queue.

THREE
I'm number three, I am you and me.
I'm not a mum, I'm just the one she works for, you see.
All over the world,
and just around the block,
in Africa and Europe too,
our mums just don't stop.
I'm number three, I am you and me.

3. Discuss the poem, drawing out the differences between the two lives. What sorts of things did 'number one' mean when she said, 'I have so much to do looking after everyone?' Do the children know anything about the lives of people, especially mothers, in the developing world? If we're all 'number three', what could we do to help 'number one' and 'number two'?

Time for reflection

Dear God,
Thank you for mums all over the world.
Thank you for the things they do to look after us and help us.
We think of mums in this country.
We think of mums in the developing world.
They all work hard.
Help us to help them in any way we can.
Amen.

Song

'Thank you, God' (*Come and Praise Beginning*, 20). Use the words, 'Thank you, God, for all our mums'.

THE LOST SON
By Judith Ayers

Suitable for Whole School

Aim

To teach the story of the Prodigal Son. To recognize the feeling of happiness when something lost has been found and the situation has been put right. To consider the concept of forgiveness.

Preparation and materials

- Two large faces drawn on card: one happy, one sad.
- Prepare the story based on Luke 15, to be read (see below) or if time permits prepare a puppet sketch or drama version (see pages 74–6), using three characters.

Assembly

1. Ask for two volunteers. Give them the drawings of faces. Ask all the children how they feel when they have lost something – sad, confused, upset. Show the sad face. Suggest different lost items for degrees of sadness, e.g. pencil, sock, lunch box, favourite toy, pet, sum of money.

   Ask the children how they feel when they have found something that they have lost – happy, relieved, pleased. Show the happy face. The more special the item lost, the happier the feeling. Go through the list of items again.

2. Read the story or perform the puppet/drama version. Tell the children that the story is written in the Bible.

   Junior's Journey
   by Gordon Lamont

   Jesus told a story about a family with two teenage sons. The parents had always said that when they died the family farm would go to both the sons, but the younger one – Junior – said, 'Can't you give me my half of the farm now? I want to sell it and enjoy the money while I'm still young.'

So that's what they did. Junior quickly sold his half of the farm and moved away to another country. He had a great time and quickly spent all his money on having fun – just think what you could buy if you had lots of money and could do what you liked with it!

Then a famine spread through that country and Junior had no money left! Not even a few pence to buy a biscuit. He'd wasted all his money and now he was hungry. Luckily he found a job looking after a farmer's pigs, but it didn't pay much money and he was always hungry – he was even jealous of the pigs who seemed to get more to eat than he did.

One morning, tired from sleeping on a hard floor, hungry, dirty and smelly, Junior woke up from a dream about his old life with his family. 'Even our servants at home were better treated than this,' he thought. 'I've been an idiot. I'll go home to Mum and Dad and my brother and tell them that I'm sorry for taking and wasting all that money. I know I can't be treated as a proper son any more – but perhaps I can be a servant, a hired worker.' He got up at once, said goodbye to the pigs and set off for home.

His father was the first to see Junior as he walked over the hill towards the family farm. Was he angry, upset, sad? No, he was happy, excited, joyful – his son had come home. All that silly business with the money didn't matter at all – his son was back. Junior had been lost, and now he was found.

There was a huge family party that night – and if you think you've ever been to a fun wild and exciting party, you should have seen Junior's welcome home party!

Only one person didn't really enjoy the party – Junior's older brother. 'It's not fair,' he said. 'I haven't wasted my money. I've been good and worked hard. I should be the one to have a party and Junior should be made to work for nothing.'

I wonder what you think?

3. Ask the children questions on the story using the happy and sad faces.

How did the younger son feel at the beginning of the story when he was working on the farm? Sad, fed-up.
How did he feel when he received his money? Happy.
How did he feel when all his money had been spent and he had nothing to eat? Sad.
How did the father feel when the son returned home? Happy.
How did the younger son feel about the way he had treated his father? Sad.
How did the younger son feel when he'd said sorry and his father had forgiven him? Happy.
How did the elder son feel when his younger brother came home and there was a celebration? Sad, angry and jealous.

If appropriate, discuss the idea of forgiveness.

Time for reflection

Ask the children to be still and quiet. Explain that when we've done something wrong and drifted away from the right way of doing things we can say sorry and be forgiven. Ask them to think of anything they have done that they are sorry for.

Dear God,
We remember that the father in the story forgives and welcomes his son home.
Help us to forgive those who hurt us.
May we never try to pay them back.
Amen.

Song

'Lost and found' (*Come and Praise*, 57)

The Lost Son – puppet/drama version

Enter Tina and Joey

Tina   Where's Gran? She promised to tell us a story.
Joey   Yeah, about the lost son. It's a strange thing to lose – I mean, you can lose your keys or your cat, but your child, your son?
Tina   I wonder what she means? I lost my cat recently. I don't know where Riki went but I was jolly glad when he came home.

Enter Gran

Gran   Hello, children.
Joey   Hi Gran, have you got time to tell us that story now?
Tina   We've been waiting for ages.
Gran   OK. Are you listening? (*Tina and Joey nod*) This is a story Jesus told and it's written in the Bible in Luke, chapter 15. Once there was a man who had two sons. The younger one was fed up working on the farm and he demanded to have his share of the farm, right now! So that he could leave the farm and spend his money on having a good time.
Joey   How ungrateful and rude.
Tina   Yes, but think of all the money he would have, while he was still young enough to really enjoy it.
Gran   The father gave his younger son his share of the farm and off he went spending the money here, there and everywhere, purely on enjoying himself, with no thought for anyone else.
Tina   If that was me I would buy lots of new clothes and have a wonderful time holidaying and partying on a cruise ship.
Joey   Trouble is, what happened when all the money ran out?
Gran   Exactly, and the money *did* run out. There was also another disaster – a famine, a severe shortage of food. So no one was able to help the young man.
Joey   Imagine that, Tina: you're on your cruise ship, no money left, the food nearly all gone, you'd have to work, probably something that no one else would do – like washing dishes for thousands of people!
Tina   Ugh, I don't think I'd like that. I might even have to eat

	the left-overs from people's plates. What did our man in the story do?
Gran	He got a job, the only thing that was offered to him, looking after pigs. He even thought about eating their food!
Tina	I think I would come crawling home, and see if my father would accept me back.
Gran	Well, that's exactly what our young man in the story did. He knew he'd done wrong and was willing to be just a hired servant on his father's farm.
Tina	He must have been feeling very sorry, and frightened about what would happen to him.
Gran	Yes, he was. It was a big thing, you know, to face up to the fact that he'd done wrong, and to realize that he needed his father's forgiveness and understanding.
Tina	I expect he crept back to the farm and hoped that not too many people would recognize him.
Gran	Well, he might have tried, but his father saw him coming. He'd been watching for him, every day since he left, hoping he'd return.
Joey	I bet he was really cross and would make him a servant and work him *sooo* hard. That would teach him.
Gran	No, his father was very pleased to see him. He ran up to him and greeted him with a great big hug and forgave him at once!
Joey	He did what?
Gran	And what's more, he instructed his servants to bring out the best robe to clothe him in and to prepare a huge feast for everyone to enjoy.

Tina and Gran start talking and arguing

Joey	(*quietly*) Excuse me. (*slightly louder*) Excuse me. (*shouts*) Excuse me! (*pause*) Can I ask a question please?
Gran	Of course, Joey, what is it?
Joey	Where was the elder son? If anyone deserved a feast he did. I mean, he'd been working hard all those years. Why wasn't there a feast for him, for being good and honest and hard working!
Tina	I bet he was very jealous and angry.
Joey	And rightly so if you ask me. The younger son should have been punished and the elder one should have had the

	party. What if it had been me that stayed at home working, while Tina went gallivanting on her cruise ship. It's not fair.
Gran	Well, the father explained it like this. He spoke very gently to his elder son and said that he had always been with his eldest son and shared everything that he had with him. But it was as if the younger son had been dead and came alive again.
Tina	Lost and found. I wonder where my cat did go when he disappeared? I never did find out how he managed to get in such a state. Oh well, I love him anyway.
Gran	Come on children, I may not have a feast, but I do have some cakes.
All	Bye, everyone.

SPIRITUALS – A BRIGHTER DAY

By Margaret Liversidge

Suitable for KS2

Aim

To encourage the children to recognize music as a positive influence in life. To explore the background and origins of 'spirituals' and 'ragtime'.

Preparation and materials

- Introductory music as the children are gathering: a piece of ragtime music by Scott Joplin, e.g. 'The Entertainer' or 'Maple Leaf Rag'.

Assembly

1. Begin with everyone singing one or two lively spiritual-type songs from the song list at the end. Afterwards, ask the children for words to describe the songs, e.g. cheerful, lively, happy, easy to sing, repetitive phrases, etc.
2. Explain that these songs have no named writer or composer. They are simply described as 'traditional'. Ask the children why they think this is so. Name the style of song as 'spiritual' and explain briefly, as follows, how they emerged from the black slave trade.

    When slaves were first captured in Africa and brought to the New World, America, they were treated very badly. They could be bought and sold as if they were animals. They were given heavy physical work to do. They were frequently beaten if they did not work hard enough.

    Many of these slaves had been taken from African tribes where people trusted in God. So, to keep their spirits up and help them work as a team – they were often chained together to prevent escape – they would sing their 'spiritual' songs which had a strong rhythm and encouraging words. Since the singing often helped them to work better, the slave masters didn't forbid it. Their songs helped to make the long hours of work more bearable.

It obviously wasn't possible for the slaves to write their songs down so they just remembered them, and passed them down through the generations. Eventually many songs were written down and recorded, so that we can still sing them today.

3. An option here is to take a drama break. Ask for four or five volunteers and guide them in miming a digging action, one behind another, digging together rhythmically. The mime could be developed to the music of one of the opening songs for a few bars.
4. Point out that we too can feel encouraged on a hard day by putting on some cheerful music, like that of Scott Joplin. Explain that some years after the slave trade had been abolished, a young black American musician called Scott Joplin continued the lively feel of black music by writing piano tunes which had a very distinctive rhythm. This type of music became known as 'ragtime'. Play some of the opening music again, perhaps running it under the reflection.

Time for reflection

Encourage the children to recognize that even today there are people who are very badly treated in some countries and so we need to be grateful that we are 'free'. Reflect on the positive effect music can have on our lives, as it did for the slaves. Their masters thought that they owned the slaves, but their music was their own and no one could take that from them.

> Father God,
> Sometimes it's just great to listen to loud music or to dance or sing.
> Thank you for giving us music.
> Thank you for music that can cheer us up when we feel low.
> **Amen.**

Songs

'I'm gonna lay down my sword and shield' (*Come and Praise 2*, 142)

'You've got to move when the Spirit says move' (*Come and Praise 2*, 107)

Other traditional spirituals, such as 'Well, you'll never get to heaven (Hand me down my silver trumpet, Gabriel)' which you may be able to find in other sources

Curriculum links

Music, History

THE WONDER OF CREATION
By Gill Hartley

Suitable for Whole School

Aim

To reflect on the unimaginable size of the universe and the incredible detail of living things.

Preparation and materials

- Read through the story in advance and have questions ready to go with the text in bold type.

Assembly

1. Ask the children what is the biggest thing they can think of. Steer the discussion towards the scale of the universe and the size of the planets and/or distances in space, etc. Ask what is the smallest thing they can think of. Encourage them to think about the intricate detail of small insects, plants, etc.
2. Tell the story of creation from Genesis 1, either in your own words or in the version below, emphasizing the infinite variety of the created world. This story is intended to be interactive! Some phrases are in bold type, indicating places where the teller should stop the story and ask the children to suggest some examples, e.g. big/small flowers, the names of star patterns (or constellations or planets), different fishes, birds or animals, etc.

How the World Began

In the beginning deep water covered the earth. There was nothing but darkness. So God said, 'Let there be light!' and it happened – there was light. God divided the light from the darkness and called one 'day' and the other 'night', and that was the first day.

On the second day, God made a vast blue and white and grey space over everything. Thin white wisps of cloud and great blue-grey banks of cloud chased around the space he called 'sky'.

On the third day, God gathered the deep water up and dry land was formed. He made narrow streams and small ponds, wide rivers and huge seas. High mountains rose up, endless deserts spread themselves out, small islands emerged and little quiet beaches came into existence. He planted tall trees, rustling grasses, and flowers of every kind – **big bright ones and tiny pale ones**. And then the third day was over.

On the fourth day, God hung lights in the sky. He put up the great fiery sun to brighten the day and the smaller gentle moon to light the night. He made thousands and thousands of **stars**, big and small, to help the moon light up the night and arranged them into **patterns** across the sky.

When the fifth day came, God looked at the earth and saw that it was empty. He made all sorts of creatures to fill the seas and rivers and ponds and streams. He made great whales, wiggly eels, minute plankton, and **fishes of every shape and size**. When he had done that, he filled the space called 'sky' with **birds of every colour**.

On the sixth day, God made animals – **furry ones and scaly ones, smooth ones and sleek ones, noisy ones and quiet ones, striped ones and spotted ones, fast ones and slow ones, great, big, huge ones and little, tiny, weeny ones!**

But that wasn't all. Then God made people. He made a man and a woman to look after all that he had made and to take care of it.

Then God looked at his wonderful creation and saw that it was very good. He smiled, and on the seventh day he rested.

3. Sing a song about the variety of the created world, from the vastness of the universe and planets to the tiny detail of the honey bee and the tree inside the acorn: 'Who put the colours in the rainbow?'.
4. After the song, ask the children to pick out from the words all the things that are big, all the things that are little and any that are neither. Ask them which is the biggest thing in the

song and which is the smallest. Remind them the created world is full of amazing variety!

Time for reflection

Say a prayer, pausing as appropriate to allow space for reflection.

Dear God,
Thank you for our world that is beautiful and awe-inspiring.
We think of the size of the universe . . .
of noisy thunder and crashing seas . . .
and we are amazed.
We look at an insect's wing . . .
the feather of a bird . . .
the patterns on a shell . . .
and we are amazed.
Our world is full of amazing shapes and sounds and colours . . .
of things big and small and huge and tiny . . .
and we are amazed at it all.
Help us to enjoy all that has been created
and to look after it with care.
Amen.

Song

'Who put the colours in the rainbow?' (*Come and Praise*, 12)

VICTORIANS – CELEBRATING THE PAST

By Kate Fleming

Suitable for KS2

Aim

To consider how life today has benefited from the past, and celebrate the courage, imagination and foresight of reformers, inventors and thinkers who laid the foundations for the modern world.

Preparation and materials

- Children may need to work in pairs with paper and pencil.
- You will need the following, or similar examples: a mobile phone, a light bulb in a lamp, connected to electricity, a photograph, antiseptic liquid.
- Prepare a flip-chart, set up as follows:

Alexander Graham Bell	Writer
Joseph Swan	Nursing
William Fox Talbot	Railway
Joseph Lister	Caring for orphan children
Florence Nightingale	Reformer/founder of National Trust
George Stephenson	Antiseptic
Thomas Barnardo	First woman doctor
Charles Dickens	Light bulb
Elizabeth Garrett Anderson	Telephone
Octavia Hill	Photograph

Assembly

1. Explain that today we are going to think about this amazing world in which we live, and particularly some of the Victorians who were brave enough, imaginative enough and clever enough to come up with new ideas which brought about much needed change in the way in which people lived.
2. Before Queen Victoria came to the throne, life in England was very different. We weren't able to do this (use mobile phone) or this (switch on light). We didn't have the joy of looking at these (show photographs) or feel the stinging of this (show antiseptic) when we graze our knees. The Victorians were responsible for telephones, light bulbs, photographs, antiseptic and many more things which today we just take for granted.
3. Introduce the game 'Victorian Match'. Explain that these famous Victorians (indicate flip-chart) are matched up with the wrong invention or occupation. Can the children help you to get the correct matches?
4. As you play – or afterwards – run through the information below. You can add extra biographical details if you have them.

> Alexander Graham Bell invented the telephone.
> Joseph Swan invented the light bulb.
> William Fox Talbot invented the photograph.
> Joseph Lister invented antiseptic.
> Florence Nightingale was the founder of modern nursing.
> George Stephenson was the engineer who built the first public railway.
> Thomas Barnardo devoted his life to caring for orphan children.
> Charles Dickens was the most famous writer of the Victorian age. His novels attacked cruelty and poverty.
> Elizabeth Garrett Anderson was the first woman to become a doctor in Britain. She founded a hospital for poor women and children.
> Octavia Hill was a reformer who worked to improve the appalling housing conditions in London. She also helped to found the National Trust in 1895.

5. All these people played an important part in the formation of modern-day society, so let's remember them and thank them when we:

> Pick up the phone to talk to a friend.
> Switch on the light or ride on the train.
> Pose for a photo.
> Graze an elbow.
> Look round a castle's turrets and moat.
> Go to the hospital, visit the nurse.
> Open the door on warm loving homes.

All these things by the kind permission of the eminent Victorians!

Time for reflection

We've so much to be grateful for today
and many people to thank.
Let us remember and salute the Victorians
who made such a major contribution
to the twenty-first century.

Songs

'Thank you for every new good morning' (*Junior Praise*, 230)
'Thank you, Lord, for this fine day' (*Junior Praise*, 232; *Come and Praise*, 32)

Curriculum links

English, History

VICTORIANS – LEARNING FROM THE PAST

By Kate Fleming

Suitable for KS2

Aim

To reflect on the past in order to consider our world today. To appreciate that contemporary thinking has been shaped by the people who lived in previous times.

Preparation and materials

- Three Year 6 children, boys or girls, to rehearse the script for performance.
- Costumes (optional) and props as necessary. This play script is set in London, but could be changed to fit any locality.

Assembly

Introduce the following scripted drama:

Scene 1: London, 1833. A cold, dark space where brothers Alfie and Davey, two chimney sweeps, are sleeping. Alfie is six and Davey is nine.

Davey   Alfie, Alfie, wake up. Mr Ruff wants us there before dawn breaks. *(shakes his brother)* We'll have to run all the way to Belgravia at this rate.

Alfie   My knees hurt, my elbow is still bleeding. Look, Davey! It's from when I helped you in that narrow chimney yesterday.

Davey   Here, look! Rub some salt into the sore bits, that'll harden the skin. You'll soon get used to it.

Alfie cries out in pain as the salt goes into his knee.

Alfie	I don't want to get used to it. I want to go back to sleep, and I'm hungry.
Davey	Come on Alfie. If we hurry Mr Ruff might have some of that plum pudding left over for us before we do our first climb. Give me your hand, little brother. Take your scraper, you're going to need that if No. 24 is how I remember it. This could well be your first climb without me, Alfie, so don't let me down, will you?
Alfie	I'll try not to, but I'm scared, Davey. It's so dark and the walls are rough and scrape my elbows and knees all the time. Sometimes I'm so frightened I can't breathe.
Davey	That'll be the fumes, only the fumes. No need to fret about that.

Both boys exit.

Scene 2: Mr Ruff, Master Sweep, is waiting in the drawing room of No. 24 Grosvenor Crescent. He has his watch in his hand. Alfie and Davey run in.

Mr Ruff	You are late, and lateness is a crime, and crime means punishment. Anyway, as I have twenty chimneys to be swept in Belgravia in the next hour, and twenty more before nine in Knightsbridge, I haven't time to punish you. It will have to wait. Now, there's a nine-inch flue in this chimney, Alfie, so as you are the smallest you'll have to go up alone. Time you did a climb without Davey.
Davey	Oh please, Mr Ruff, I don't think he's ready. Let me go up first, or at least let me go up with him. He's only little, and his knees and elbows are bleeding and raw. His breathing was bad this morning, and he's frightened, Sir.
Mr Ruff	He's been up with you since I bought him, and it's well time he went up on his own. I can't afford to have you both up there, and you are too big now to do nine-inchers. Up you go, Alfie.

Alfie exits. Davey watches him climb from the fireplace.

Davey	Go on, Alfie, you'll be all right. Keep knocking with your scraper so I know where you are. He's doing

	well, Mr Ruff. He's not too far away from the flue. Slant your body, Alfie, like I taught you. Bend yourself to fit the flue.

Sounds of knocking.

Mr Ruff	He needs to make haste. Davey, you start on the dining-room chimney. Old misery-guts Grimshaw the housekeeper is waiting, she needs to get breakfast going in there soon for his Lordship.
Davey	Please let me wait, Mr Ruff, to make sure Alfie's all right. He is my brother, and I promised Mother when you bought him that I'd look after him. Alfie! Knock if you're through the nine-incher.

Silence.

Davey	Alfie! He's trapped in the nine-incher and can't get his breath, Mr Ruff! I'm going after him.
Mr Ruff	Oh no, you're not. I don't want to lose two of you.
Davey	(*desperate shout*) ALFIE!

End freeze-frame as Davey turns to look at Mr Ruff.

Discuss the drama with questions and comments such as: Poor Alfie stuck in the nine-incher. Hopefully Davey can save him. What do you think? What kind of a job were Alfie and Davey doing? Was that a long time ago? How many years ago? Who was Queen at that time?

That time was called the Victorian period. Some children had to do all kinds of work from a really young age. Alfie was six and Davey was nine.

Point out that there were people in Victorian times who thought that it was wrong to make children go up chimneys, down mines, and work in factories. So they worked tirelessly to put a stop to it. They wanted children to go to school, live healthy lives, and enjoy being young. Just like you do.

If we look back, as we have done today, we can see that life is much better for many children in the UK now than it was in Victorian times. It is important to look back into history and reflect on the past. This helps us to handle the world we live in and not make the same mistakes either now or in the future.

Finish by saying that the children might like to continue the story in their own way, in drama, writing, dance or storytelling.

Time for reflection

History helps us to improve our society and gives us important evidence with which to shape our ideas and attitudes.

> Dear God,
> Please help us to do what we can for the improvement of our world,
> and to help those who are less fortunate than ourselves.
> **Amen.**

Songs

'Thank you, Lord, for this fine day' (*Junior Praise*, 232; *Come and Praise*, 32)
'Thank you for every new good morning' (*Junior Praise*, 230)

Curriculum links

English, History, PSHE

WISE OR FOOLISH – MAKING CHOICES

By *Margaret Liversidge*

Suitable for KS1 or Whole School

Aim

To illustrate how making wise choices can affect our circumstances in life.

Preparation and materials

- Read through and prepare the story below.
- Introductory music as the children are gathering: 'Accentuate the Positive' (available on BBC CD *The Singing Detective*).

Assembly

1. Verbally play a game of opposites with the children, where you give a word and the children should come up with the appropriate opposite, e.g. black/white, day/night, fat/thin, tall/small, high/low, wise/foolish.
2. Relate to some of the above and explain that opposites can be like the choices we make in life; if we choose to paint a door bright yellow it will look very different from one that is painted dark blue.
3. Introduce the story of the wise man and the foolish man as a parable, a story with a special meaning. This story can be found in Luke 6.47–49. Encourage the children to repeat after you the words in bold:

   Once there were two men. Each decided to build himself a new house. They both looked around for a place to build.

   The first man was in a hurry; he wanted to have his new house straightaway. So he started to build right where he was

standing, on a flat sandy place. In no time at all his new house was finished. He looked out of the door and said, '**That didn't take very long to build, I'm going to be very happy living here.**'

But the second man was troubled. He looked at the rolling clouds in the sky. He knew that the rains were coming soon. He climbed up a steep hill, away from the flat, sandy soil. He decided to build his new house on a high, rocky place.

His house took a long time to build. Every day he watched the clouds grow darker. Then one day he put away all his tools and went indoors. '**That took a long time to build, I'm going to be very happy living here.**'

The neighbours admired both of the new houses. Then they looked up at the thunder clouds. '**How wise you are,**' they said to the second man; then they ran for shelter!

4. Sing verse 1 of the song, 'The wise man built his house upon the rock'. Ask the children what happened to the house the wise man built and why – he chose carefully, he was a man who was wise enough to make good choices.
5. Sing verse 2 of the song. Ask what happened to this house and why – he made a bad choice.

Time for reflection

Tell the children again that this Bible story is called a parable because it has a special meaning. Jesus compared himself to a rock. He explained that people who believe and trust in God are making a wise choice, like the wise man in the story.

Spend a few moments encouraging reflection on 'making choices', i.e. in relation to life at school. Remind the children that wise choices usually lead to good/positive outcomes and foolish choices can lead to bad/unhappy outcomes.

Sometimes we don't know what is the wisest thing to do – that's when we need to stop and think, talk to other people and to ask God for help. Just what the foolish builder should have done.

> Dear God,
> Help us to make wise choices,
> when we are working in our classes,

when we are playing with our friends,
when we are living in our homes.
Amen.

🎵 Song

'The wise man built his house upon the rock' (*Junior Praise*, 252; *Kidsource*, 336)

STRONGER TOGETHER

By Tom Bayliss

Suitable for Whole School

Aim

To emphasize the importance of working and praying together.

Preparation and materials

- A chair (with a suitable hole or handle at the top for lifting), and a reel of cotton. Test out the practical element of the assembly beforehand!

Assembly

1. Place the chair at the front with you and ask for a volunteer – someone who thinks they are strong enough to lift up the chair. When the person comes to the front, tell them that they are to lift up the chair with a single thread of cotton, by passing the cotton through the hole/handle at the top and lifting the cotton with their hands. (The cotton should break – make sure the chair is not so light that it lifts!)
2. Repeat the experiment with two strands of cotton, then with three, four, five, etc., until the chair does lift and the cotton doesn't break. Perhaps ask the watching children whether or not they think it will lift each time.
3. Explain that although a single strand of cotton couldn't do the job, several strands together could. Talk about how sometimes in life we have difficult things to do or hard decisions to make. Quite often we cannot do them on our own. The Bible teaches us that there is great strength to be had in praying for each other, and in sharing each other's problems. More importantly, the Bible teaches us that we are never alone, for Jesus is always with us and he will help us every time we ask.

Time for reflection

Dear God,
Sometimes life is full of happy things, sometimes life is difficult.
Thank you for my friends who share things with me and help me.
Thank you that wherever I am and whatever I am doing,
you are always there for me and you are always ready to listen.
Amen.

Song

'It's the springs' (*Come and Praise*, 82)

EASTER 1 – TURNING THE TABLES
By Jill Fuller

Suitable for KS2

Aim

To explore the character of Jesus. To explore anger and its links with justice.

Preparation and materials

- Choose and prepare for reading or retelling a version from one of the four Gospels of the story of Jesus turning over the tables in the Temple. In Matthew 21.12–14 and Luke 19.45–48 this event appears as one of the incidents during the week before Good Friday which is customarily called Holy Week. In Mark 11.15–19 and John 2.13–17, the story is positioned nearer the beginning of Jesus' ministry. Use an easy-to-understand version such as the Good News Bible, or a children's Bible may offer a helpful alternative version. The version from Luke is included below.

Assembly

1. Ask the children if they have ever been really angry. Ask them to share one or two experiences. Is there a difference between being angry because we can't get our own way and being angry because something really isn't right or fair? Can they think of a story in which Jesus was angry?
2. Explain that the following story probably happened during the week leading up to Easter. Remind the children that Jesus had just entered Jerusalem on a donkey. Crowds of people came to see him and cheered him as a hero. Many powerful people were worried about how popular Jesus had become and some didn't like his teaching.

3. Explain that the Temple in Jerusalem was a place of pilgrimage, especially at the time of the Passover. People would bring offerings, often of animals, as symbols of thanksgiving or of sorrow for past sins. These animals could be bought at the entrance to the Temple. It seems likely that the people who sold the animals, the money-lenders or merchants of the story, were charging too much and cheating the poor. Jesus may have heard about this, although that is not recorded in the Gospels. Ask the children to listen carefully to the story and think about the following: how they think Jesus is feeling, what Jesus does, and what he says.
4. Read the story or tell it in your own words.

> Then Jesus went into the Temple and began to drive out the merchants, saying to them, 'It is written in the Scriptures that God said, "My Temple will be a house of prayer." But you have turned it into a hideout for thieves!' Every day Jesus taught in the Temple. The chief priests, the teachers of the Law, and the leaders of the people wanted to kill him, but they could not find a way to do it, because all the people kept listening to him, not wanting to miss a single word. (Luke 19.45–48)

5. Ask the children: How do you think Jesus was feeling? What did he do? What did he say?

   Was Jesus putting himself in danger by expressing his anger? Discuss whether the children are surprised to hear a story in which Jesus expresses anger. Why do they think he was angry? Are there times when it is right to show we are angry? Is it right to be angry about injustice or unfairness? What was Jesus trying to change by his anger?

Time for reflection

Think about a time when you have been angry. Was it right to be angry?

> God of all creation,
> Help us as we try to understand all our feelings.
> Help us to recognize when we are angry
> and to see when things we do or say make other people angry.

Help us to see the difference between anger that is selfish and anger that seeks justice for others or ourselves.
Help us to choose our actions with care, courage and love.
Amen.

Song

'To everything turn, turn, turn' (*Come and Praise*, 113)

Curriculum links

- English: Use the story as the basis for drama. Collect vocabulary around the experiences of anger.
- RE: Begin a zigzag book, class newspaper or frieze depicting the events of Holy Week.
- History: Explore the lives of social reformers whose anger or 'passion' against injustice helped others.
- Art: Explore how children might paint pictures to express anger.
- Music: Explore composing or listening to music that suggests anger.
- SMSC: In circle time use explorations such as 'I feel angry when . . .' and 'I cope with feeling angry by . . .'

EASTER 2 – CARRYING THE CROSS
By Jill Fuller

Suitable for KS2

Aim

To think about helping others and being a good neighbour by looking at the character of Simon of Cyrene.

Preparation and materials

- You will need two assembly leaders, one to introduce Simon and conclude the assembly, and the other to tell the story of this brief episode 'in role', through the eyes of Simon.
- Background information: read Mark 15.21–22 (the Good News Bible version is below). Cyrene was a Greek city where many Jews lived. It was situated on the north coast of Africa, the capital of modern day Libya. Perhaps Simon was living outside Jerusalem and was visiting the city for the Passover. He is named as the father of Rufus and Alexander. In his letter to the Romans, Paul sends greetings to 'Rufus, that outstanding worker in the Lord's service, and to his mother who has always treated me like a son' (Romans 16.13). Perhaps this was the same Rufus.

> On the way they met a man named Simon, who was coming into the city from the country, and the soldiers forced him to carry Jesus' cross. (Simon was from Cyrene and was the father of Alexander and Rufus.) They took Jesus to a place called Golgotha, which means 'The Place of the Skull'. (Mark 15.21–22)

Assembly

1. Leader 1 recalls with the children the events that happened after Jesus shared the Passover (the Last Supper) with his

disciples. Jesus is betrayed by Judas, is arrested in the Garden of Gethsemane and abandoned by the disciples. He faces trials before the chief priests, Pilate the Roman governor and King Herod.

Finally Pilate presents Jesus to the crowd, asking them who they want freed – Jesus, or Barabbas, a murderer. They shout for the release of Barabbas. Pilate washes his hands and condemns Jesus to death on a cross.

The soldiers torture and mock Jesus. They give him the cross to carry through the streets of Jerusalem to Golgotha, a hill outside the city, where the Romans put criminals to death by crucifixion. Introduce Leader 2, 'Simon', who will tell the next part of the story.

2. Simon tells his story. Remember to include:

   The walk to Jerusalem, expecting to take part in the Passover.
   The unexpected jostling of the crowds on the way to the crucifixion.
   Seeing the exhausted young man falling under the weight of the cross.
   The soldiers grabbing Simon and telling him to carry the cross.
   Simon's fear and concern for his own sons, Rufus and Alexander. Would they get lost in the crowd?
   The weight of the cross.
   Arriving at Golgotha.
   The effect of the event on himself and his sons.

3. Leader 1 discusses with the children how Simon helped Jesus by carrying the cross when Jesus was weak and in need. Point out that Christians, and many people, think that part of being fully human is to be ready to help each other and 'share each other's burdens', to be a good neighbour.

Time for reflection

Think about Simon.
He was in town with his family for a festival.
He didn't want to get caught up in the bad things that were happening.

But Simon saw someone who needed help . . .
And he gave it.

Think about the day ahead.
Will there be ways that you can help another person in need today?

Song

'When I needed a neighbour' (*Come and Praise*, 65)

Curriculum links

- English: Use the story as a basis for imaginative writing as the character of Simon or Rufus.
- RE: Using the Gospel accounts, make a diary of the events on that Thursday and Good Friday.
- History: Find out about the work of a Roman soldier.
- Art: If possible look at some depictions of the Stations of the Cross in art or by a visit to a local church.
- Music: Listen to a short passage from a choral work about the crucifixion.
- SMSC: Discuss times when children have 'carried crosses' by helping each other.

EASTER 3 – SUNDAY MORNING

By Gordon and Ronni Lamont

Suitable for Whole School

Aim

To tell the story of the resurrection.

Preparation and materials

- The assembly takes the form of the story of the first Easter Sunday with join-in actions. They might not all be appropriate for all age groups, so be prepared to adapt. One approach is to get a group of 'actors' to come to the front to 'ham it up'; or the whole assembly could join in from where they sit. However you organize it, it's a good idea to have another teacher leading the actions while you tell the story. Treat it as a fun event, going back over particularly enjoyable parts.

Assembly

Explain that you are going to tell the story of a special Sunday morning a long time ago, and that everyone will need to join in to make the telling complete.

It's very early in the morning – dawn. You're up and about, but it's so early . . .
Everyone yawns.
You're going to visit a garden and a tomb in the garden. It's cold and a bit spooky in the early morning light.
Everyone shivers.
Suddenly there's a huge earthquake.
Everyone jumps and shakes.
And a flash of bright light.
Everyone shields their eyes.
Before you know it, there's an angel standing right in front of

you – an *angel*. There are guards at the tomb and they begin to tremble.
Everyone trembles.
Then the guards fall down in a faint, as if they're dead.
Everyone makes feeble fainting noises.
The angel rolls away a huge stone from the entrance to the tomb – just rolls it away like it's a football. The angel speaks to you and tells you not to be afraid. 'The person you're looking for isn't here any more – he has been raised from the dead.'
Then he's standing right in front of you – your friend, who was dead, is alive again. You're amazed, can't believe it, astounded.
Everyone acts astounded – open-mouthed amazement.
Your friend says, 'Peace be with you' and 'Don't be afraid'. Your friend was dead.
Everyone drops his or her head.
And now he's alive again.
Everyone looks up.
Give him a clap, such a clever chap.
Everyone claps.
Shhh, don't wake up the guards!

Time for reflection

Dear God,
Thank you for that first Easter day.
Thank you that the stone was rolled away.
Thank you that our friend came back to stay.
Starting on that first Easter day.
Amen.

Song

'From the darkness came light' (*Come and Praise*, 29)

Summer Term

PSALM 150 – A SONG OF PRAISE
By Jill Fuller

Suitable for Whole School

Aim

To introduce the concept of the psalms. To explore Psalm 150 with its theme of praise.
Note: This assembly shares the same general introduction to the psalms as that on Psalm 19 (see page 13).

Preparation and materials

- You will need a Bible large enough to be seen easily by everyone.
- Practise reading Psalm 150, or rehearse a child to read it. The Good News Bible version is included below. You can of course use another translation.

Assembly

1. Hold up the Bible and ask the children if they know what it is called. Explain that the one book, the Bible, is really a collection of many smaller books. Explain that there are two main sections and ask children if they know what these are called (Old Testament and New Testament).
2. Explain how the Old Testament tells mainly the story of the Jewish people before Jesus, and the New Testament tells the story of the life of Jesus and also contains letters and describes events in the early Christian Church.
3. Say that today we are looking at a book in the Old Testament called The Book of Psalms. The Hebrew title of the book, *sepher tehilim*, means 'book of praises'; the English word 'psalm' comes from the Greek word *psalmoi* meaning 'songs accompanied by string music'.

4. Use some of the following information to explain about the psalms:

   The Book of Psalms is rather like a hymnbook. Just as a hymnbook contains songs and hymns written at different dates, so the psalms were written at different times in Old Testament history.
   There are 150 psalms. We do not know for sure who wrote them. People think there were many authors, but generally David, the shepherd boy who fought Goliath and later became king, is thought to have written about half of them.
   It is likely that the psalms were usually sung and sometimes accompanied with music. In the Hebrew text, a word meaning musical interlude, *selah*, often occurs (e.g. Psalm 46).
   The psalms were used in worship both at the Temple in Jerusalem and in synagogues (explain Jewish places of worship if necessary). Jesus would have known the Book of Psalms.
   The early Church probably used psalms in public services. They are still used today by both Jewish and Christian people in synagogues and churches.
   The psalms are almost like talks with God, and contain many moods. Sometimes the writer is joyful and full of praise and trust, at others desperately sad and questioning God.

5. Introduce Psalm 150 as a psalm praising God. Ask the children to listen carefully as the psalm is read to the ways the psalmist thinks of praising God (a variety of instruments and dance). Read the psalm.

   > Praise the Lord!
   > Praise God in his Temple!
   > Praise his strength in heaven!
   > Praise him for the mighty things he has done.
   > Praise his supreme greatness.
   > Praise him with trumpets.
   > Praise him with harps and lyres.
   > Praise him with drums and dancing.
   > Praise him with harps and flutes.
   > Praise him with cymbals.
   > Praise him with loud cymbals.

Praise the Lord, all living creatures!
Praise the Lord!

6. Sing 'Praise the Lord in everything' (*Come and Praise*, 33). Ask the children to note how music, dancing, poetry, acting, and caring for others and all things, can be ways of praising God.

Time for reflection

In a moment of quiet, ask children to reflect on ways in which their actions, work and play can be a 'psalm of praise' during the day.

You may choose to end with the responses, 'Let us praise God', 'Thanks be to God'.

Song

'Praise the Lord in everything' (*Come and Praise*, 33)

Curriculum links

- English: Write a psalm of praise.
- RE: Special books – explore how the Bible came to us.
- Art/DT: Choose a psalm, or a verse from a psalm, to write out and illustrate or decorate around the edge.
- Music: Listen to the various ways psalms have been set to music by different composers, e.g. *Come and Praise*, 33 and 54, Byrd, Taizé, Iona, John Rutter.

TUMMY ACHE
By Ronni Lamont

Suitable for KS2

Aim

To use a Gospel story of healing (Mark 5.25–34) to explore the idea of wholeness.

Preparation and materials

- Bottles of medicine, pills, etc.
- Vitamins.
- A bowl of fruit, some vegetables and a bottle of milk.
- Quiet music, with a peaceful feel – e.g. Enya.

Assembly

1. Begin by asking the children if they've ever had tummy ache. Lots of them will have had a 24-hour bug, or variations. Ask them how they felt. How does tummy ache make you walk? Would you like to always have a tummy ache?

2. Tell the following story about a woman who had tummy ache for 12 years. Right low down, all day and all night.

    What would you do if you had tummy ache and it wouldn't go away? See the doctor – and so she had. In the time that she lived, you had to pay to see a doctor, and she'd spent all the money she had, but it didn't get better.

    It got so that she lived all on her own, and people didn't want to talk to her. They walked round her in the street, in case they caught it. The people didn't want to sell food to her in case they caught it.

    Can you imagine how sad she was? Put on the music, if you are using it, at a low volume.

3. Ask the children to shut their eyes, and think about that

woman: the pain in her tummy, the sadness at no one wanting to be kind to her, no one being her friend. Ask the children to spend a few moments with their eyes shut, thinking about the woman who had a bad tummy ache for 12 years, and imagining how she must have felt.

4. Keeping their eyes shut, ask them to imagine how it feels if someone tells you that there's a man called Jesus, and he might be able to make you better. Can you feel your heart leap with hope, and excitement? Straightaway, you walk to the town where he is. Keep your eyes shut and listen. Can you hear the excited crowd shouting 'Jesus, Jesus'? In your imagination, go to the crowd.

    And then you realize that you can't ask him to make you better. It would be too awful if they pushed you away, told you to leave him alone. So you gently creep round the back, to touch the edge of his clothes.

    And as you touch his clothes, you know that you're better! The tummy ache is gone – but Jesus swings around and asks, 'Who touched me?'

    What can you do? You don't want to own up, and besides, lots of people are crowding round. It may not have been your touch that Jesus felt.

    But you know it was. Slowly, you stand up straight, and walk round to face Jesus.

    What does he look like? Is he tall? Looking down crossly at you, or is he looking at you kindly, smiling?

    He simply says, 'Your faith has healed you', and tells you that you can go. And you do. You go home, and thank God for being well again.

5. Now open your eyes. How did you feel when you realized you were better? How did you feel when you heard Jesus calling for you? What was it that made you well?

6. Show the objects you have with you – the medicines and pills. When do we need these? (When we have an illness.)

    What about the fruit and veg and milk? We eat and drink these to keep us well. Explain that we have to make an effort to keep ourselves well. We need to do our bit so that we don't get ill as often as we might.

    And when we are ill, we take our medicine and that helps to heal our bodies.

Often, when someone is ill, other people pray for them to be made better. It's good to hold people in love, to be aware of caring about them. We ask Jesus to heal them, as he did the woman who touched his clothes. Usually it takes a bit longer, though!

Sometimes they don't get better, and that's very hard, and very sad. But the woman in this story did get well – and she probably told everyone for ages afterwards how she was made better.

Time for reflection

Lord, help us to look after ourselves the best we can,
to eat well, and to take exercise.
Help us when we are ill to be patient
and wait for our bodies to get better.
Bless the nurses and doctors,
and everyone who looks after people who are sick.
In a quiet moment, think about anyone you know who is ill.
Ask God to help them.
Amen.

Song

'Kum ba yah' (*Come and Praise*, 68)

LIGHT AND DARKNESS
By Gill Hartley

Suitable for Whole School

Aim

To celebrate the joy of light after darkness.

Preparation and materials

- A candle and matches.
- A copy of *Can't You Sleep, Little Bear?* by Martin Waddell. The big book format would be best (Walker Books, ISBN 074453691X).

Assembly

1. Introduce the use of the candle in religion to the children. If it is not a regular feature of school assemblies, explain that all sorts of people who believe in God light a candle when they are going to pray to show they are doing something special.
2. If possible, make the hall dark by switching off lights and drawing any curtains. Light the candle. Ask the children to think about how they feel as they look at the candle.
3. After a few moments ask the children to share how they feel (if they wish to). Does the candle make them feel good or bad? Is light a good or bad thing? (The responses are invariably positive!)
4. Blow out the candle. Ask if any of the children are afraid of the dark. They don't have to own up if they do not want to, but assure them that many people are and that it is acceptable to be so.
5. Read the story *Can't You Sleep, Little Bear?* by Martin Waddell and show the pictures as you do so.
6. Ask the children what it was that made Little Bear feel better.

Emphasize that it was the light. He went through a whole series of lights, each one bigger than the last, until he found one big enough to comfort him.
7. Sing the song, 'From the darkness came light'.

Time for reflection

If appropriate, point out to the children that the song they have just sung refers to Jesus as Light. Read the words of Jesus in John 8.12:

> Again Jesus spoke to them, saying, 'I am the light of the world. Whoever follows me will never walk in darkness but will have the light of life.' (NRSV)

Song

'From the darkness came light' (*Come and Praise*, 29)

Curriculum links

Science, Literacy

ANTONIO VIVALDI
By Margaret Liversidge

Suitable for Whole School

Aim

To encourage children to recognize the value of having a positive attitude.

Preparation and materials

- A board or card showing the words 'Antonio Vivaldi 1678–1741'.
- Flip-chart/OHT and pen.
- If possible, some seasonal pictures, i.e. spring, summer, autumn, winter.
- 'Spring' from Vivaldi's *Four Seasons* as listening music at the beginning and end of the assembly.

Assembly

1. Comment on the different expressions on the children's faces as they are sitting listening to you speak at the beginning of the assembly. Ask for a volunteer to come out and draw on the flip-chart a face with a positive expression. During and after the drawing, ask the children to interpret how a person is feeling when they are wearing a positive expression. Repeat the exercise, but this time with the emphasis on a negative expression/feelings.
2. Explain that we can be influenced by the positive or negative attitudes of other people/children and that it is a good thing in life to learn to develop a positive attitude in as many situations as possible, for our own benefit but also for that of others.
3. Refer to the composer Antonio Vivaldi's name. Explain how he was strongly influenced in life by noticing the natural

world around him. If he had been an artist he might have painted beautiful pictures. If he had been a poet he might have written descriptive poems. But since he was a musician, he wrote beautiful music, which painted descriptive pictures through the very clever use of sounds.
4. Vivaldi was always looking for ways of creating new musical sounds. In his compositions he experimented with the sounds using many different instruments and voices. Ask the children to listen carefully for the way Vivaldi has used instruments to recreate bird sounds in 'Spring', the listening music for this assembly/week.
5. Vivaldi's music is always energetic, full of life and never old-fashioned. Explain that, for these reasons, some adults are able to recognize Vivaldi's music when they hear it played. A bright and cheerful day could be referred to as a 'Vivaldi Day'. At this point (or earlier) look together at the seasonal pictures you may have and relate them to Vivaldi's musical interpretation of nature. Comment on how noticing and appreciating the world around can cheer us up and help us change our attitude.
6. 'A cheerful heart is good medicine' (Proverbs 17.22). Ask the children to think about this saying. What do they think it means?

Time for reflection

Ask the children to consider their attitude today. Could they aim to show a positive face to the world, even if they are feeling negative? Encourage them to realize that being positive affects both themselves and others.

If the sun is shining, thank God for a 'Vivaldi Day'!

> Lord of all cheerfulness,
> please help us to have a positive attitude towards our work,
> our teachers and helpers,
> our play and our friends today.
> **Amen.**

Songs

'God of the morning' (*Come and Praise 2*, 105)
'All things bright and beautiful' (*Come and Praise*, 3)

Curriculum links

Music, PSHE, Art

FEELING SAFE
By Gill Hartley

Suitable for Whole School

Aim

To explore the parable of the lost sheep (Luke 15.4–7) in relation to friendship and feeling safe.

Preparation and materials

Read through the story in advance of the assembly.

Assembly

1. Ask the children if there has ever been an occasion when they have known they were lost (for instance in the supermarket when they were very little) or even when they have just been separated from their carer for a short while. Can they remember how it felt? And how did it feel when they were found and safe again?
2. Tell the story Jesus told of the lost sheep, emphasizing how the sheep might have felt, as in the version below:

The Lost Lamb

There was once a shepherd who had a flock of one hundred sheep. In the shepherd's flock there were all kinds of sheep, big and small, young and old, white and speckled. There was one sheep in particular, a small speckled lamb called Ben, who was always getting into trouble. He never wanted to stay with the rest of the flock where he was safe, but wanted instead to go off exploring the big wide world beyond.

Every morning the shepherd led his sheep out of their pen and up the hillside to find fresh grass to eat. At the end of the day he would collect them all together and walk them back down to the pen where they would be safe for the night. When he got to the gate of the sheep pen he would count each sheep in to make sure they were all there.

One particular evening when they arrived back and the shepherd was nearing the end of his counting, he had a shock. 'Ninety-seven, ninety-eight, ninety-nine . . .'

Where was the hundredth sheep? It was nowhere to be seen!

Meanwhile Ben was still up on the hillside. He had decided that today was the day he would finally explore the big wide world. When all the other sheep began to move off down the hillside at the end of the afternoon he hid behind a rock and watched them go. When they were out of sight he skipped off further up the hill to see what he could find.

He paddled across a stream, chased a sparrow round a bush and raced a bee on its way back home. He was so busy having fun that he didn't watch where he was going. Suddenly he fell down into a hollow and landed in a bramble bush!

He stood up to scramble out and found that he was stuck fast. His woolly coat was caught on the brambles and he couldn't move. He began to feel scared. It was getting dark and he was all alone. He wanted to be safe with the other sheep, not stranded up on the hillside unable to move. There might be wild animals around! He was frightened and began to bleat.

After what seemed like hours, Ben thought he heard something. He listened more carefully. Yes, there it was again. It was the shepherd's voice calling to him! Within minutes the shepherd was gently freeing him from the brambles. How glad Ben was to see him and how happy he was to be lifted up onto the shepherd's shoulders and taken back down the hillside to the rest of the flock and the safety of the sheep pen.

3. Explain that Jesus told stories like this one to help people to understand what God is like. In this story the shepherd searched and searched to rescue his lost lamb and take it back to the safety of its pen. Jesus wanted people to understand that God is like the shepherd who cares about his sheep.
4. Sing the song, 'Lost and found'.

Time for reflection

Reread the last verse of the song, asking the children to think about what it means to them. When we're lost or scared or frightened, having a friend there with us can help us feel safe again. Stress the importance of staying close to our adult carer(s) and being sure that we know where they are and they know where we are. We don't want to be like Ben the sheep – lost, alone and frightened! For many people, God can be 'the friend who is very near . . . who takes away our fear.'

> Dear God,
> Keep us, and all whom we love, safe from harm today and every day.
> Watch over those who are in any kind of danger.
> Help us to be good friends to those who are scared or frightened.
> And thank you that you can help us when we are afraid.
> **Amen.**

Song

'Lost and found' (*Come and Praise*, 57)

MAKING THINGS

By Gordon and Ronni Lamont

Suitable for Whole School

Aim

To celebrate the joy of creativity.

Preparation and materials

- A blackboard or flip-chart.

Assembly

1. Ask if there are any Lego fans in the assembly. Ask a few volunteers to describe their favourite models. Do the same for a number of other creative activities, such as drawing and painting, writing, making things out of old boxes, and making scrapbooks.
2. Explain that today we're thinking about the idea of creativity – making things and making things up. Explain that this can include any type of activity where you put things together – Lego bricks, words, old boxes – to make something new.
3. Explain that you are all going to be creative this morning – you're going to think up something to do with the theme to fit each of the letters of the word CREATE. Then ask the children to come up with ideas for the first letter, C, and all the others in turn (use the given sentence for the second E, below). Write them down as you go along. Some suggestions are:

    C cardboard boxes, card, colouring, craft, cartoons, composing
    R radio-controlled models, resin modelling, retelling stories, robots
    E excitement, entertaining, engineering, edibles, enthusiasm

A art, acting, activities, assembling, acrobatics
T theatre, toys, tube of glue, trinkets, telling stories
E Everywhere I go, in everything I see, wonderful, exciting creativity is all around me.

4. Ask the children to consider the following words, the very first words from the Bible: 'In the beginning God created . . .' Explain that many people believe that the gift of creativity is one of the most precious – to be able to make things and make things up is something that God wants all of us to do.

Time for reflection

In the beginning God created. Today we create – with words and cardboard models, songs and acting, bricks, and in so many other ways.

> Dear God,
> Thank you for your special gift of creativity.
> Thank you that everywhere I go,
> in everything I see,
> wonderful, exciting creativity is all around me.
> **Amen.**

Song

'If I had a hammer' (*Come and Praise*, 71)

PILGRIMAGES
By Jill Fuller

Suitable for Whole School

Aim

To introduce and explore the notion of pilgrimage.

Preparation and materials

None.

Assembly

1. Discuss with the children the idea of having a place that is special to them. Do they have one? Is there somewhere they like to go to be quiet or alone, a secret spot?
2. Explain that there are some places that are special to groups of people: football stadiums such as Wembley, homes of pop stars, such as Gracelands, the home of Elvis Presley, war memorials, churchyards with family graves.
3. Explain that just as individuals, families, clubs and schools have special places that they like to visit, so do some religious groups. Often the places they visit have a special memory of their God or of a special saint.
4. Explain that Hindus make a special journey to the source of the River Ganges, Muslims visit Mecca, and Jewish people go to Jerusalem. Point out that people often make the journey either because they want to express thanksgiving to God, or to ask forgiveness when they think they have done wrong. Explain that these special journeys to special places are often called 'pilgrimages' and the people who make the journey are called 'pilgrims'.
5. Explain that there are many places of pilgrimage in this country: for example, Canterbury, with the shrine of St

Thomas Becket; Salisbury, with the shrine of St Osmond; Holy Island and Iona.

6. Talk about how in times past people would have made long journeys and bought special 'pilgrim' badges to pin on their hat or cloak. They would have travelled in a group and would perhaps have a special prayer request to make in the church at their destination. Sometimes they would light candles and leave them at the special place.

Time for reflection

In a moment of quiet, imagine that you have travelled to a special place of pilgrimage. Think of why you have come to this place – is there something you want to say thank you for? Is there something you want to say sorry for? Is there something you want to ask God for?

Say your own prayer, in your head, or just think for a moment about why you've made your special journey – your pilgrimage.

> Dear God,
> Thank you for all the special journeys to special places
> that people make all over the world,
> and have made throughout history.
> Thank you that there are so many special places in the world
> – so much to see.
> Thank you that pilgrims make their journeys with other people,
> and so make new friends as they journey together.
> **Amen.**

Song

'He who would valiant be' (*Come and Praise*, 44). Explain that the words of this song are by John Bunyan, who wrote a story about a pilgrim – *The Pilgrim's Progress*. The words are quite difficult but the line at the end reminds us that we are all pilgrims on the very special journey of life.

Curriculum links

- English: Look at a short extract from *The Pilgrim's Progress* or *The Canterbury Tales*.
- RE: Find out about places of pilgrimage.
- Geography: Find places of pilgrimage on a map of the UK.
- Art: Look at designs of pilgrim badges and create new ones.

ALONE – SOMETIMES I WANT TO BE ON MY OWN

By Kate Fleming

Suitable for Whole school

Aim

To look at the good things about being alone, and the way in which this enhances being with others.

Preparation and materials

- Read through the story and poem in advance.

Assembly

1. Introduce the story about a boy called Jason.

   Jason gazed out of the window and watched the rain as it trickled down the window pane and splashed into the puddles. A wet Saturday morning – goodie, he could stay in his room and play with his friend Humphrey. Humphrey was imaginary, and had been his friend for as long as he could remember.

   Hurried footsteps on the stairs signalled the arrival of his mother. 'What a miserable day,' she said. 'Now, who can we get round to play? You don't want to be on your own, do you? What about Sean? You like him, don't you? Or Mahinda, or Edward, or Johnny Macpherson, his mum is so lovely, or Robbie, Amerjit, Gregory?'

   'I think I'm OK, thanks Mum, I'll stay here on my own today.'

   'You'll be lonely, Jason, bored and fed up. There's nothing worse than having nothing to do, and nobody to play with.' She stood there in the doorway with that determined look on her face.

'I'm not lonely, bored, or fed up, Mum, there's so much to do up here; you really don't have to worry about me.'

Reluctantly she left the bedroom and clattered downstairs, shouting out, 'Jason, you'll be sorry!'

Jason smiled, 'Lonely? There's loads to do in my bedroom. Finish my book, work out the last bit of the Lego truck, sort out my Pokémon figures and cards! All this with the help of Humphrey.'

Humphrey, Jason's oldest friend, began life as a dog on wheels, and had played a major part in helping Jason to master the complex art of walking at the age of one. He had grown with Jason and was now a sophisticated and worldly nearly nine year old who wasn't quite as good at Pokémon as Jason was!

They played happily, read together, completed the truck, and put all the Pokémon figures and cards in swapping order – there would be no stopping him now!

The sound of the telephone broke the silence. The bedroom door swung open.

'It's Sean's mum. Do you want to go over this afternoon to play football, now the rain has stopped?' his mother asked, phone in hand.

'Yeah! That would be great, I fancy a game of footie with Sean!'

But I wouldn't have missed being alone this morning, thought Jason, as he picked up his football kit and raced down the stairs.

2. So Jason, in our story, found that sometimes it's good to be on your own, and sometimes good to be with other people. Ask the children: Jason liked to read and play with his Lego. What kind of things do you like to do on your own? Jason liked to play football with his friend Sean. What kind of things do you like to do with other people?
3. Ask the children: Are there times when you don't like to be on your own? Are there times when you don't like to be with other people?
4. Explain that Jason had thought about being alone and being with other people. He chose to write a poem about how he felt. This is Jason's poem.

Sometimes I like to be on my own,
reading a book or simply thinking about things.
Sometimes I like to be with my friends,
and enjoy all the fun and excitement that brings.

Sometimes it's great to have my friends round,
setting up camps, or watching TV.
Then when it's time for them to go home,
I'm back once again with my family.

You might like to write your own poem about being on your own and being with your friends when you go back to your classroom.

Time for reflection

Dear God,
Thank you for all my friends and family.
Help me to enjoy the time I spend on my own,
and the time I spend with friends and family.
Amen.

Reprise the poem if appropriate.

Song

'Thank you, God, for all our friends' (*Come and Praise Beginning*, 20). Add 'Thank you, God, for time alone'.

Curriculum links

English, PSHE

SAMUEL IN THE TEMPLE – LISTENING TO GOD

By Ronni Lamont

Suitable for Whole School

Aim

To help children to think about the different ways in which we experience God.

Preparation and materials

- Allocate part of the assembly area as the Temple where Eli and Samuel sleep.
- Ask a teacher to play the part of God (to say 'Samuel, Samuel').
- Learn your 'script' well in advance, so that you are able to keep the drama moving on. The story is found in 1 Samuel 3.

Assembly

1. Explain that we are going to think about a really old story from the Bible today, about a boy who was about seven years old when this happened. Ask two children to come out, one to take the part of Samuel and one to be Eli.
2. Explain that Samuel lived with Eli in the Temple (like a large church). Samuel's Mum and Dad came to visit him every year, but he was learning how to be a priest, looking after God's house.
3. Tell and enact the story.

   It's night-time, so Samuel and Eli are asleep, in different rooms in the Temple. (*Ask Samuel and Eli to lie down in different areas.*)

   In the middle of the night, Samuel hears someone calling.

(*The teacher calls*) 'Samuel, Samuel'. So Samuel gets up, and goes to ask Eli what he wants. (*Samuel goes over to Eli and wakes him up.*)

But Eli says it wasn't him calling: 'Go back to bed, Samuel and leave me to sleep.' So Samuel does as he is told. (*Samuel goes back to his bed area, and goes back to sleep.*)

Then it happens again: 'Samuel, Samuel'. Samuel again wakes up Eli and asks what he wants. 'It was you, Eli, I heard you call.' Once again, Eli says it wasn't him.

4. An option at this point is to break off from the story and ask the children how you think Eli is feeling, having been woken up twice. How do their mums and dads react if they wake them up twice in quick succession?
5. Continue the story.

Eli wonders just what's going on here. He decides on a strange plan of action. He says to Samuel that if he hears the voice again, to say, 'Speak Lord, for I am listening.'

Samuel goes back to bed, and they both go back to sleep.

And the voice comes again: 'Samuel, Samuel'. But this time, Samuel sits up in bed and says – what? (*Ask the children and then get Samuel to say it.*)

And who was it who was calling Samuel? It was God. And God told Samuel lots of things, and that was the beginning of a very special friendship between Samuel and God. Samuel went on to be very important in the story of the Jewish people. But he never forgot how God called him, when he was just a little boy, asleep in the Temple.

Thank the children and let them go back to their places.

Time for reflection

How do we hear God speaking to us? (There may be no answers to this question.)

When we go out for a walk and look at the beautiful world, is that God being with us?

What about when we feel excited at taking part in or watching sport?

When we know we've done something wrong, is that God?

Where can we go to hear God? Perhaps somewhere quiet, where we can concentrate on what's going on inside of ourselves.

God rarely speaks to people as he spoke to Samuel, but if we are quiet and we listen, we learn to recognize God speaking in all sorts of ways.

Help me, God, to hear you speaking to me.
Help me to learn how to listen to you,
and to recognize your voice in the world.
Amen.

Song

'Kum ba yah' (*Come and Praise*, 68)

Curriculum link

RE

BREATH AND BREATHING
By Patrice Baldwin

Suitable for KS2

Aim

To raise the children's awareness of their own breathing. To learn that breathing air is essential to life. To reflect upon the fact that we all share the same air through breathing many times.

Preparation and materials

- An empty jam jar and a piece of cloth to conceal it.
- A balloon.

Note: Your attention is drawn to the phrase in the Time for reflection: 'Every person and living creature will one day breathe their last breath'. You may wish to omit this if there are children who have recently suffered bereavement.

Assembly

1. Hold up the empty jam jar covered by the cloth. Tell the children that the jar in your hand contains something very precious. Ask the children what it might be and gather suggestions. You could give some riddle clues:

    It's something that we use all the time.
    It's something that everybody needs and shares.
    It is free.
    It's something we borrow and give back.

    Try to build up some dramatic tension. Ceremoniously remove the cloth to reveal the empty jar, and say, 'Here it is!' The children may think the jar is empty or may realize that it is full of air. Confirm that it has air in it.
2. Take the balloon from your pocket and blow it up. Ask the

children what the balloon contains. Whose air is in the balloon? They will probably say yours. Let go of the balloon so that it releases the air. Whose air is it now? Emphasize that we share the air. It belongs to nobody. It enters our bodies but we let it go again.
3. Ask the children to close their eyes and to keep their bodies comfortable and still so that they can concentrate on their breathing. Ask them to breathe in through their noses and out through their mouths. They should take long, steady, controlled breaths.
4. Try to move towards synchronizing their breathing so that all the children breathe in and out in unison, according to your instructions. On the in breath you could say 'We take the air' and on the out breath 'We give it back'. Repeat this several times.

Time for reflection

Ask the children to be still and quiet, listening as you guide their thoughts (pausing at times for reflection and so that they can be aware of their own breathing).

> We breathed our first breath when we were born and we gave it back . . .
> Through our lives we breathe many breaths . . .
> We share the air with each other many times . . .
> Every person and living creature will one day breathe their last breath . . . they breathe their last breath and they give it back . . .
> At every moment a baby somewhere is breathing its first breath . . .
> The air gives us life and we give the air back for everyone.

Finish with a few moments of silent reflection, allowing the children time to focus silently on their breathing, before they reopen their eyes.

Songs

'Deep peace' (*Come and Praise Beginning*, 23)
'Kum ba yah' (*Come and Praise Beginning*, 24), adapting the

verses, e.g. 'Someone's breathing, Lord, Kum ba yah'.
'Peace be in our waking' (*Come and Praise Beginning*, 25), substituting 'breath' for 'peace'.

> ### Curriculum links
> - Science: Life and living processes – the human body.
> - Music: Composition based on the rhythm of breathing.

PERSEVERANCE
By Gill Hartley

Suitable for Whole School

Aim

To reflect on the need to keep going even when things are difficult.

Preparation and materials

- Something unfinished, e.g. a piece of writing, a piece of craftwork, a picture.
- A large piece of paper with the word PERSEVERANCE written on it.

Assembly

1. Show the children the piece of unfinished work you have brought with you. Ask them why they think it isn't finished. Talk about ideas such as not enough time, too hard, got bored, ran out of materials, intend to finish later, etc.

    Ask if they can remember something that they didn't finish. Why didn't they finish it? How did they feel about not finishing it? You will probably receive a variety of answers to this question! Hopefully someone will indicate the idea of feeling unhappy or dissatisfied.

2. Take the children through the following imaginative exercise:

    Close your eyes and imagine you are in your classroom . . .
    You are doing a piece of very difficult work . . .
    It's so difficult you don't think you can do it . . .
    You ask your teacher for help . . .
    S/he tries to help you . . .
    You go back to your table and try again . . .
    It's no good, you still can't do it . . .

Your teacher says, 'Keep trying – you can do it!'
What does it feel like? Is it easy to keep trying?

Share some of the children's answers.

3. Ask them if they know the word for keeping going even when things are really difficult and all they want to do is to give up. Show them the word PERSEVERANCE.
4. Sing a song about keeping going: 'One more step along the world I go'.
5. Ask the children to pick out words from the song which are about perseverance (keeping going), such as, 'Give me courage when the world is rough'.
6. Introduce an extract from a poem which says something about perseverance: 'Uphill' by Christina Rossetti. Ask the children to think about the words as you read them.

> Does the road wind uphill all the way?
> Yes, to the very end.
> Will the journey take the whole day long?
> From morn to night, my friend.

Point out that some things in life are 'uphill all the way', and some just seem like it.

Time for reflection

Dear God,
Help us to keep trying even when things are difficult –
it's so easy to start and then give up if things are hard.
Help us to ask for help when we're stuck
and to find the courage in ourselves to have another go.
Amen.

Song

'One more step along the world I go' (*Come and Praise*, 47)

LOOKING AFTER GOD'S WORLD – OR 'NAME THAT JOB!'

By Jeff Graham

Suitable for Whole School

Aim

To help children understand that we all have a responsibility to look after the world, and that all jobs and tasks have value in the eyes of God.

Preparation and materials

- Six small cards, each showing the name of a task the school caretaker does with which the children are familiar, for example vacuuming, dusting, picking up litter.
- Prepare six children to do short mimes of the tasks. Show them the cards before the assembly.
- A sheet of sticky labels, each showing 'I am a caretaker' or 'I am a caretaker of God's created world'.
- It would be good if the school caretaker were prepared to answer questions. If not, you need a flip-chart or OHT.
- Music: 'What a Wonderful World!' sung by Louis Armstrong.

Assembly

1. Tell the children that there is a very important task for all of us in this world. Say that in a few minutes you are going to read a few lines about this from the Bible, but first some people are going to mime some activities that take place in school. Ask the children to try and work out what each job is, but keep it to themselves for now.
2. One by one the six mimes are demonstrated. After all have been done, ask the rest of the children what they considered

each task to be. Can they think of one person in the school who does all these tasks? When the word 'caretaker' is offered, affirm this, and if the caretaker is in the hall, ask him or her to come and sit at the front. Tell the children that Mr/Mrs 'X' in the hall (someone who is not the school caretaker) is a also caretaker (pause and put a sticker on him or her). Then say that Mr/Mrs 'Y' in the hall is another caretaker (pause and put a sticker on him or her). Then say to a few other named people in the hall, 'Z', you may not know it, but you are a caretaker too, and so are you, 'A' (put stickers on them too).

3. Go on to say that God wants us all to 'take care' of the world he created. Then read or paraphrase, and give context to, the Bible verse Genesis 2.15.

   > Then the Lord God placed the man in the Garden of Eden to cultivate it and guard it.

4. Ask the school caretaker what she or he considers to be the best bits about the job. What makes him or her happy (e.g. being creative, making the school a brighter place)? What are the worst parts of the job? What makes him or her feel sad (e.g. picking up litter, getting rid of graffiti)? If the caretaker is not available, ask the children to consider these things and record positive and negative items on the flip-chart or OHT.

5. Then invite responses or make statements about the activities that people do that harm the world, and those that improve or benefit the world. Remind them that God wants us all to 'take care' of the world, and that we can all start with how we look after our school and neighbourhood.

Time for reflection

Play 'What a Wonderful World!' sung by Louis Armstrong and ask the children to close their eyes and imagine the wonderful scenes he describes.

> Dear God,
> Help us to take care of, and appreciate,
> the wonderful world you created for us.
> **Amen.**

As the children leave, play the music again and ask them to think about their favourite parts of the school, the locality, the world.

♪ Song

'Morning has broken' (*Come and Praise*, 1)

PULLING TOGETHER
By the Revd Alan M. Barker

Suitable for Whole School

Aim

To show the need for co-operation, and to consider that every contribution to shared effort can be vital.

Preparation and materials

- Seven children are needed to perform the drama. The performers gradually form a chain by taking hold of one another as the story is narrated. Audience participation can be invited; ask everyone to give the encouragement to 'PULL' after the phrase 'they pulled'. The narration may be undertaken by the assembly leader, or other children.
- Some animal masks or face paints could be used to portray the dog, cat, and mouse.

Note: There is a useful Bible link to this assembly: 1 Corinthians 3.5–10 (servants of God). Paul and Apollos were both church leaders. Some people thought that one was more important than the other. However, Paul says that everyone has a part to play in God's work: 'We are partners working together for God' (verse 9).

Assembly

1. Introduce the theme with a reminder of the popularity of DIY (do it yourself). Ask the children if they can think of any DIY tasks that one person can do by themselves: e.g. decorating, furniture assembly, gardening. Ask whether they have ever helped with a DIY task. Can they think of any tasks that are too big for one person to undertake alone? (e.g. constructing a garden shed, building a house extension, carrying heavy items).

2. Point out that while some tasks can be achieved by one person working alone, others require the help and energy of a number of people working together. Co-operation is vital. Explain that this is so in many areas of life, as the following story shows.

The Story of the Enormous Turnip

Once upon a time, a man sowed some turnip seed in his garden. After some days it began to grow, but one seed grew faster that all the rest. It grew and grew, and did not stop growing, until the leaves were like a bush and the most enormous turnip had formed beneath the ground.

The time came when the man decided to pull up the enormous turnip to eat. Going to his vegetable patch he rolled up his sleeves and took a firm grasp of the stems. Then he pulled (PULL!), and he pulled (PULL!), and he pulled (PULL!). But he couldn't pull up the enormous turnip.

So he called to his wife: 'Please can you come and help me?' She took hold of his waist and together they pulled (PULL!), and they pulled (PULL!), and they pulled (PULL!), but still they couldn't pull up the turnip.

So the wife called to her son: 'Please can you come and help us?' So the son took hold of his mother and together they pulled (PULL!), and they pulled (PULL!), and they pulled (PULL!), but still they couldn't pull up the turnip.

The son then called to his sister: 'Please can you come and help us?' So together they pulled (PULL!), and they pulled (PULL!), and they pulled (PULL!), but still the enormous turnip remained in the ground.

A friendly dog stopped at the garden gate. The girl called out: 'Please will you come and help us?' So the dog came and gently took hold of her dress. Then they pulled (PULL!), and they pulled (PULL!), and they pulled (PULL!), but still the enormous turnip would not budge.

By now everyone was getting very hot and tired. When a cat walked down the path the dog barked: 'Please will you come and help us?' Taking hold of the dog's tail, the cat joined in. They pulled (PULL!), and they pulled (PULL!), and they pulled (PULL!), but they couldn't pull up the enormous turnip.

Just then a mouse scuttled out from underneath the hedge, and instead of chasing it, the cat meowed: 'Please will you come and help us?'

'A mouse!' exclaimed the others. 'A mouse! What difference will a mouse make?'

But the mouse cautiously took hold of the cat; and the cat took hold of the dog; and the dog took hold of the girl; and the girl took hold of the boy; and the boy took hold of his mother; and the woman took hold of the man; and they pulled (PULL!), and they pulled (PULL!), and they pulled (PULL!), and again with all their might they pulled (PULL!). And suddenly the enormous turnip flew up from the ground and they all tumbled in a heap!

The man and his wife carried the turnip to the house and used it to cook a vegetable stew. And at suppertime there was more than enough to eat for every one of them. Even the dog and the cat and – don't forget! – the mouse!

3. What does this story tell us? That when we meet with a huge challenge and are faced with a big task, it's important to pull together. The effort of everyone is important and the smallest help can make all the difference.

Time for reflection

Dear God,
Help us to learn to work together.
May we never be too proud to ask for help, nor too hesitant to give it.
Thank you for the ways in which we will help (have helped) one another today.
Amen.

Songs

'Give me oil in my lamp' (*Come and Praise*, 43)
'Fill thou my life' (*Come and Praise*, 41)

TRY YOUR BEST – DON'T WORRY!
By Margaret Liversidge

Suitable for KS2

Aim

To enable children to recognize that everyone can feel anxious about exams and tests and that the best approach is simply to 'try your best'.

Preparation and materials

- OHT or flip-chart and pens.
- Introductory music as children are gathering: track from *Rhythm of Peace*, or *Moods: the Magic of the Panpipes* or other similar calming music.

Assembly

1. Launch straight into the assembly in story-telling mode:

   James could hardly believe it. His teacher was actually in a good mood. She must have had a very good weekend – she hadn't mentioned revision or tests for at least an hour! Mrs Roberts was speaking:

   'This morning, children, I have two tasks for you. First I would like you to make up as many acrostics as you can using the letters T, E, S, T, for TEST. Put your hand up when you've thought of a good one and it doesn't matter about your spelling, we can sort that out later.'

   James could hardly believe his ears. They were actually going to make a joke out of tests. Hands began to shoot up all around the room.

   'Tests Exist Simply for Teachers,' said Sarah.

   'These Exceptionally Stupid Tasks,' shouted Callum and Joe.

'Tricky Exams Smell Terrible,' said James, and everyone laughed.

Mrs Roberts then explained to the class what they were going to do next. 'We're going to use the "Tests Secrets" box which I've made for you. I'd like everyone to write anonymously on a piece of paper – what does "anonymously" mean, Mahinda?'

'It means you don't put your name on it, Mrs Roberts.'

'Quite right, Mahinda. So you're all going to write how you really feel about tests and then we will post what you have written in the box. You can begin your sentences with "I think that . . ." or "I feel that . . ." and you can write as many comments as you like.'

It was then that James felt his heart sinking, his hands felt sweaty and a lump rose in his throat. 'Why do I have to feel like this every time we talk about tests?' he asked himself.

2. Ask the children what they thought about the idea of the Tests Secrets box. Then ask for suggestions as to what some of the sentences might be that Mrs Roberts would find in the box. List on the OHT or flip-chart the children's key words/phrases, both positive and negative, which may be suggested, e.g. worried, excited, dreading, afraid, etc.

3. In discussion, focus specifically on James. Encourage the children to describe how James was feeling physically. Explain that when we are anxious, the human body can naturally react in these ways. Such symptoms of anxiety are not unusual and it doesn't mean we are ill or different from others. Mention that adults too can feel worried about tests or exams, but worry can also have a positive effect, spurring us on to work hard and do our best.

4. Enable the children to explain how James was feeling emotionally – refer to the word list where relevant. Explain that others in the class shared James' concerns but because we are all individuals, no two children will react in exactly the same way.

5. Apply the issues that have arisen, with the emphasis on seeking help from parents and teachers and discussing any concerns the children may have. Explain that adults might not realize how children feel unless they are actually told.

Emphasize that the most positive thing we can all do is to aim to 'try our best'. Remind the children that they mustn't let themselves down by not working hard and doing what they are capable of, but having tried their best, they can be satisfied and relieved to know that their best efforts will be appreciated.

Time for reflection

Write the key words 'try your best' for the children to be aware of during the time for reflection. Ask them to consider how they feel about tests. Explain that negative feelings can become positive ones if they focus on 'try your best'.

Explain that some people find it helpful to tell God how they are feeling, and ask for God's help. Refer to 1 Peter 5.7: 'Leave all your worries with him, because he cares for you.'

> Father God,
> Thank you that you care about all our feelings and you never give up on us.
> Please help us to think positively about all our schoolwork and about tests.
> Help us to remember to always try our best.
> **Amen.**

Song

'The wise may bring their learning' (*Come and Praise*, 64)

Curriculum link

PSHE

WORDS AND HOW WE USE THEM
By Jill Fuller

Suitable for KS2

Aim

To help children to appreciate the power of words, for good or ill.

Preparation and materials

- A large dictionary and a candle.
- Have ready some tongue twisters of varying difficulty for the children to try to say or ask them to prepare some in advance, e.g. Bertie Bear bought big blue balloons; Tamsin trickily tried to toss ten trays of treacle toffees; thirty swallows swooping through swaying willows swished their wings.
- Prepare one or two children to tell jokes, or trust to your luck and ask on the day! Alternatively just use the tongue twisters.
- Be prepared to share an example of being hurt by words or ask the children to think about examples from their own lives, books they have read or TV/radio situations.

Assembly

1. Show the children the dictionary and ask someone to explain what it is full of and what it is used for.
2. Discuss with the children all the ways we use words: to express opinions and feelings, to give instructions, to describe an event, to exchange news, to tell jokes, etc.
3. Share the tongue twisters and jokes with the children, giving time to enjoy the experience of playing with words.
4. Ask if they have ever been hurt by words and if possible give a personal example of being wounded by words. Give

opportunities for the children to identify when words have been used to bully, taunt or spread unkind rumour.
5. Discuss how the words we use can affect the way others feel about themselves. We can use words for humour, for encouraging, comforting, and affirming each other, or for destroying self-confidence and spreading rumours.
6. Read Proverbs 12.18: 'Gossip can be sharp as a sword, but the tongue of the wise heals.'

Time for reflection

Light the candle and ask the children to reflect in a moment of silence on the way they will choose to use words during the day. You may like to conclude the time of reflection with the following verse:

> Let the words of my mouth and the meditation of my heart be acceptable in thy sight,
> O Lord, my rock and my redeemer. (Psalm 19.14)

Song

'Peace, perfect peace' (*Come and Praise*, 53)

Curriculum links

- English: Making a book of tongue twisters. Work on alliteration.
- Maths: Graphs of use of different languages across the world.
- Science: Looking at speech and sound waves.
- RE: Special words. The special books of the major world faiths.
- History: How words change and develop through history, e.g. 'posh', from 'port out starboard home'. The development of books and printing.
- Geography: Awareness of distribution of languages across the world.
- Art/DT: Using printed words to create a collage picture. Painting a picture in response to a particular word, e.g. anger, peace, war, care.

- Music: Word rhythms. Composing a rap.
- SMSC: Development of school rules about how words are used and courteous ways of replying to others. Discussion about freedom of speech.

SCHOOL SPORTS
By Gill Hartley

Suitable for KS2

Aim

To celebrate Sports Day and to consider the similarities between life and running a race.

Preparation and materials

None.

Assembly

1. Talk to the children about the school Sports Day, either recalling the last one or anticipating the next. Ask them what races and events there were/will be on Sports Day. Who likes running? Who is good at running? Who is better at something else?
2. Introduce the word 'athlete' to the children, if it is one they do not know already, and then tell the following story.

Racing Against Time

On a warm afternoon in May nearly fifty years ago, three men stood together on a running track in Oxford and looked up at the sky. They were glad it was a fine day, but they weren't so pleased with the wind that was blowing. That could spoil their plans completely!

Two of the men were called Chris – Chris Chataway and Chris Brasher – and the third was called Roger Bannister. They were all athletes and they had come together that day to try to break a record. They wanted to do something that some people thought was impossible – they were going to try to run a mile in less than four minutes.

Athletes nowadays have set records for running a mile in well under four minutes, but at that time no one had ever managed to run it that fast. For several years, athletes had been trying and they had managed four minutes eight seconds; and then four minutes six seconds; and even four minutes two seconds; but never less than four minutes! Some people said it couldn't be done.

But on 6 May 1954, Roger Bannister was going to try. He and his friends waited all day, anxiously watching the weather and hoping the wind would stop. Just after five o'clock in the afternoon it seemed the wind had died down enough to give it a try. Roger Bannister set off, with his two friends.

Each lap of the running track was a quarter of a mile, so they had four laps to do. Roger ran the first in less than a minute – that was good, he was on target! The second lap was completed in just under two minutes – still on target! But at the end of the third lap the time was just over three minutes. That meant he had to complete the last lap in well under a minute if he was to achieve the four-minute record.

His two friends had been running by his side to pace him so that he could run his fastest. Now Roger summoned up all his determination and energy. He quickened his pace, his friends were left behind and he pounded over the last few yards of the track. As he went through the finishing tape there was a burst of cheering, and then there was silence. Had he done it? What was his time? Was it under four minutes? The voice of the announcer broke the silence. 'Time', he said, 'three minutes, fifty-nine point four seconds.'

Roger Bannister had done it! The noise of the cheering was deafening! Roger Bannister had achieved the impossible! All his training and determination had paid off! Roger Bannister became the first man to run a mile in less than four minutes.

3. Explain that you are going to read out some words about running races written by a famous Christian teacher over nineteen hundred years ago and written down for us in the Bible. Read 1 Corinthians 9.24–26, either from a modern version of the Bible, or use the paraphrase below:

In a race everyone runs, but only one person gets first prize. So run your race to win. To win the race you have to give up things that stop you doing your best. An athlete goes to all this trouble just to win a ribbon or a silver cup; but in life we do it for a reward in heaven. So I run straight to the finish with determination in every step.

Tell the children that these words are from a letter written by a man called Paul to some people who had only recently become Christians and were still learning how they should behave. Paul is telling them that life is a bit like running a race – they will need a lot of determination and training to do their best.

Time for reflection

Dear God,
Thank you for the joy of running,
for the fun of races and thrill of doing well.
We know that not everyone can win a race,
and we cannot win every race we run,
but help us to do our best.
Help us to train to run the race of life
and give us the determination to do our best always.
Help us to live today in such a way
that everyone who meets us is glad to do so.
Amen.

Song

'He gave me eyes so I could see' (*Come and Praise*, 18)

Indexes

Index of Authors

Ayers, Judith 71
Baldwin, Patrice 22, 130
Barker, The Revd Alan M. 138
Bayliss, Tom 93
Fleming, Kate 31, 39, 47, 60, 62, 83, 86, 124
Fuller, Jill 6, 13, 28, 34, 95, 98, 105, 121, 144
Graham, Jeff 135
Hartley, Gill 3, 10, 17, 37, 66, 80, 111, 116, 133, 147
Kazer, Barbara 8
Lamont, Gordon and Ronni 43, 53, 69, 101, 119
Lamont, Ronni 24, 100, 127
Liversidge, Margaret 19, 57, 77, 90, 113, 141

Index of Biblical References

Genesis 1.1—2.4 80; 2.15 135; 8.22 6; 9.12–15 6
1 Samuel 3.1–18 127
Psalms 19 13; 150 105
Proverbs 17.22 113; 12.18 144
Daniel 3 24
Matthew 2.1–12 53; 14.22–23 34; 19.13 34; 21.12–14 95
Mark 1.35 34; 5.25–34 108; 6.41 34; 11.15–19 95; 14.32–33 34; 15.21–22 98
Luke 5.16 34; 6.47–49 90; 10.25–37 8; 15.4–7 116; 15.11–31 71; 19 3; 19.45–48 95
John 2.13–17 95; 8.12 111
Romans 16.13 98
1 Corinthians 3.5–10 138
1 Peter 5.7 141

Index of Themes and Content

Actions/activity
All together now! 37; The Bible 66; Gift tags 28; Making things 119; Stronger together 93; Victorians – Celebrating the past 83

Attitudes
Alone 124; Bravery 10; Gift tags 28; No room . . . 43; Perseverance 133; Stronger together 93; Try your best 141; Why worry? 1 60; Why worry? 2 62

Bible
The Bible 66; The cook's tale 47; Easter 1 95; Easter 2 98; Easter 3 101; Epiphany 53; Feeling safe 116; The Good Samaritan 8; Light and darkness 111; Looking after God's world 135; The lost son 71; New school year 3; No room . . . 43; Prayer 34; Psalm 19 13; Psalm 150 105; Pulling together 138; Samuel in the Temple 127; The seasons and God's promise 6; Shadrach, Meshach and Abednego 24; Try your best 141; Tummy ache 108; Vivaldi 113; Wise or foolish 90; The wonder of creation 80; Words and how we use them 144

Children's lives
Families 31; Mums 69; New school year 3; School sports 147; Tummy ache 108

Culture
All together now! 37; Football 17; Making things 119; Pilgrimages 121;

Spirituals 77; Victorians – Celebrating the past 83; Victorians – Learning from the past 86; Words and how we use them 144

Drama
The Good Samaritan 8; Easter 3 101; Families 31; Looking after God's world 135; The lost son 71; Mums 69; Pulling together 138; Samuel in the Temple 127; Shadrach, Meshach and Abednego 24; Victorians – Learning from the past 86; Why worry? 160; Wise or foolish 90

Faith element
The Bible 66; Easter 1 95; Easter 2 98; Easter 3 101; Epiphany 53; Feeling safe 116; Football 17; Handel 19; The lost son 71; New school year 3; No room . . . 43; Pilgrimages 121; Prayer 34; Samuel in the Temple 127; The seasons and God's promise 6; Shadrach, Meshach and Abednego 24; Spirituals 77; Wise or foolish 90

Famous people
Handel 19; Mozart 57; Vivaldi 113

Music
Bravery 10; The Good Samaritan 8; Handel 19; Mozart 57; New school year 3; Spirituals 77; Vivaldi 113; Water 22; Why worry? 1 60; Winter 39

Nature
Breath and breathing 130; Looking after God's world 135; Water 22; The wonder of creation 80

Seasons
The seasons and God's promise 6; Winter 39

Story
Alone 124; The cook's tale 47; Easter 1 95; Easter 2 98; Easter 3 101; Feeling safe 116; The lost son 71; School sports 147; Try your best 141; Tummy ache 108; Wise and foolish 90; The wonder of creation 80

Visual aids used
Bravery 10; Breath and breathing 130; Epiphany 53; Families 31; Football 17; Handel 19; Light and darkness 111; The lost son 71; Mozart 57; Perseverance 133; Prayer 34; Psalm 19 13; Psalm 150 105; The seasons and God's promise 6; Tummy ache 108; Vivaldi 113; Water 22; Winter 39

Whole school
All together now! 37; Alone 124; The Bible 66; Bravery 10; Easter 3 101; Epiphany 53; Families 31; Feeling safe 116; Gift tags 28; The Good Samaritan 8; Handel 19; Light and darkness 111; Looking after God's world 135; The lost son 71; Making things 119; New school year 3; No room . . . 43; Perseverance 133; Pilgrimages 121; Prayer 34; Psalm 19 13; Psalm 150 105; Pulling together 138; Samuel in the Temple 127; The seasons and God's promise 6; Stronger together 93; Vivaldi 113; Water 22; Why Worry? 2 62; Winter 39; Wise or foolish 90; The wonder of creation 80